WHAT
THE BIBLE
TEACHES
ABOUT
JESUS

WHAT THE BIBLE TEACHES ABOUT

JESUS

Geoffrey W. Grogan

SERIES EDITOR: G. W. KIRBY

Tyndale House Publishers, Inc. Wheaton, Illinois

Unless otherwise stated, biblical quotations are from the *Revised Standard Version* of the Bible.

Library of Congress Catalog Card Number 79-64982. ISBN 0-8423-7884-7. Copyright © 1979 by Geoffrey W. Grogan. First published in Great Britain by Kingsway Publications, Ltd. Tyndale House edition published by arrangement with Kingsway Publications, Ltd. All rights reserved. First Tyndale House printing, July 1979. Printed in the United States of America.

CONTENTS

64007

INTRODUCTION
The man who is always news

People are fascinating. Julius Caesar, Francis of Assisi, Leonardo da Vinci, Garibaldi – there is a quartet of interesting and varied personalities you might study for years, and just from one country's history! 'The proper study of mankind is man,' so they say, and we shall never exhaust that study.

One man stands above all others. Jesus, a carpenter, reared in an obscure town not even mentioned in his nation's literature before his day, has placed his grip upon the minds and hearts of people in a quite special way. His character and personality have fascinated all kinds of folk for two thousand years. More books have been written about him than about any other human being. His life and the documents which record it have been subjected to scholarly research more intense than that devoted to any other life or record. All this tempts us to rephrase the old saying so that it reads, 'the proper study of mankind is *the* Man.'

We are living in times of great change, and the greatest changes of all are taking place in people's outlook and life-style. Despite this there is no sign that the interest in Jesus is waning. Just the reverse. The film *Jesus of Nazareth*, screened in two three-hour (yes, three-hour!) parts on British television at Easter 1977, drew enormous audiences. Whatever we may think of their theology, *Godspell* and *Jesus Christ, Superstar* were great box office successes. The book *The Myth of God Incarnate* presents an interpretation of him that many of us find quite unacceptable, but we knew from the start that it would arouse great interest. At the height of their fame, the Beatles were quoted as saying, 'We are more popular than Jesus.' Time has a wonderful way of cutting down such claims to their proper size.

It is striking how many leaders of other religious groups have found the life and character of Jesus especially interesting. Jews like Klausner and Montefiore, Hindus like Gandhi, and many others, have been deeply impressed by him and his teaching, even though they have not become Christians. Even those who have written against traditional ideas of him have left their own testimony to his uniqueness. David Strauss, a sceptic if ever there was one, declared: 'Christ stands alone, and unapproached in the world's history.' Ernst Renan, another sceptic, called him 'the Incomparable Man', and said of him, 'Between you and God there is no longer any distinction.'

Jesus' influence has been incalculable. We cannot over-estimate the extent of it on the history of civilization and human nature. W. G. de Burgh in *The Legacy of the Ancient World* analyses the sources of modern civilization. Egypt, Babylon, Persia and others have each made their own contribution but there are just three major sources – Greece, Rome and Israel. The influence of the latter finds its focus in one man – Jesus of Nazareth. The history of western art cannot be understood at all without a study of the Christian faith. The exciting world of science owes far more to impulses arising from him than is often recognized. A Muslim parent once approached his son's headmaster with a complaint. There was no proper Christian religious education in the school and so his son was not getting the education he needed. 'But,' replied the astonished head, 'I thought you were a Muslim, not a Christian!' 'Certainly,' said the father. 'We are a Muslim family and we intend to stay that way, but we are immigrants, not just birds of passage in this country. How is my son ever going to understand Britain and the British unless he understands the religion that has moulded their culture all these centuries?'

Jesus of Nazareth has been changing people's lives ever since he came into the world. The New Testament tells the story of lots of them. He does it still. We might expect to meet such people in church, but many readers of this book will have met them in the home, at school, in the factory or the office. We might expect to hear them make their witness during gospel radio broadcasts, but they sometimes turn up on *This Is Your Life* or *Down Your Way*.

In short he is the man who is always news. All sorts of editions of Bible books are circulating now. Perhaps nothing was more appropriate than the idea of putting one of the gospels out in the format of a newspaper. How can a man who is dead be news? Christians give an immediate answer to this. He is not dead. He is alive! He rose from the dead! He is our 'Great Contemporary' and he is working today just as he did in Palestine, except that he now does his work over a much wider area – and the New Testament shows us that this is exactly what the first Christians believed.

It is time we turned to these documents and looked at their account of the facts.

1

JESUS IN THE BIBLE
Presenting the Facts

This book explores what the Bible has to say about Jesus of Nazareth. If we want to know what he was like (and therefore what he is like) this is the only method available. Why? Because the Bible contains the primary documents, and every historian knows this is where to begin. Here I shall take it for granted that the writers were telling the truth about him. This does not mean there is no place for asking if the gospels are historically accurate. There are plenty of good books on the market which seek to vindicate the historicity of these writings. This, however, is not our purpose just now.

Do you need particular views of biblical inspiration to profit by this book? No. Just give the biblical writings the kind of respect primary documents deserve and normally receive. Nor does this mean that questions of inspiration are unimportant. It does mean you can get somewhere with the Bible witness to Jesus without starting off with a particular view of Scripture. It is worth remembering that these men had been wonderfully changed by Jesus Christ. Would this not give them a new concern for truth? In fact Christians have found the Bible witness to be remarkably self-consistent. Accepting it has had far-reaching effects upon many lives.

The Bible is a big book. Let us start with Mark, the simplest of the gospels. A volume like the present one should never be treated as a substitute for Bible study, but as an aid to it. You will therefore get most out of it if you start by opening the Bible *now* at the gospel of Mark. Even better, read the gospel through first and then study the comments.

Mark

Mark defines his purpose in the first verse of his book. He is really a preacher bringing us good news about Jesus. Jesus is the Christ, the Son of God. These titles mean he is God's promised King (promised, that is, to the Jews in the Old Testament) and that he has a special relationship with God himself. Because he was promised, we are not surprised to find his forerunner, John, introduced with Old Testament quotations. As God's King Jesus is endowed with God's Spirit, and as God's Son assured of his favour.

A king in ancient times was his people's war-leader. Already in the first chapter the great enemy Satan makes his appearance, and we see we are to witness a conflict. Jesus shows his kingly authority, not only over nature (the wild beasts) but also over the evil spirits – Satan's agents – and over all kinds of disease.

He comes, however, not only to cast out demons and heal the sick but also to preach and call for a verdict ('repent; believe'). He begins to gather followers, for a king has a right to make his authority felt. In fact enormous crowds are attracted to him. Out of these followers he selects twelve for personal training, so that they may preach his message and exercise authority as his men.

We see more and more that the enemy has many human agents. These are not only in expected quarters – for example among the Herodians, the supporters of 'King' Herod who has no divine right to authority – but also among the religious leaders of the people, the scribes and Pharisees and even, in Judas, within his own following. In fact chapters 2 and 3 show him in spoken conflict with the religious leaders on issue after issue. He clearly believes it is his right to clarify important questions about man's relationship with God and the interpretation of the Old Testament, even though this puts him against the most respected theologians of his day.

In chapter 4 there is a pause in the rapid succession of events as God's King explains in picture language some basic principles of the kingdom, but the action starts up again at the close of chapter 4. A king is called to save his people. This king is divine (4:41, 'Who then is this...?') and so in four very different situations he shows his power to save people when they are clearly beyond human help. Chapter 6, however, shows us that men can only know him as the Saviour-King if, setting aside all prejudice, they will believe in him and receive his messengers, whether these are his disciples or his forerunner.

Just as Israel needed not only to be saved from Egypt but given God's provision in Canaan, so Jesus, as the Shepherd-King, is Provider as well as Saviour. This is made abundantly clear in two miracles of feeding. In fact, references to food are so frequent in chapters 6–8 that Mark must surely be making some emphatic point here. Part of this passage, including the story of the feeding of the four thousand, concerns events outside purely Jewish territory (7:24–8:10). He came to save and feed men everywhere.

What have the disciples been doing up to now? They have been with him, listening and watching, but not always understanding. Jesus' reference to this is followed by the fascinating and unique miracle of the blind man given sight in two stages (8:22–26). This seems like an acted parable (what a marvellous sense of positioning Mark has, to be sure!) for it introduces the great confession of his messiahship by Peter but also the same disciple's refusal to listen to some most unpalatable teaching. The disciples now know he is God's Christ; they have yet to realize that the ecclesiastically approved 'Christology' they have learned from childhood is all wrong. (Incidentally *Christ* and *Messiah* are Greek and Hebrew equivalents, and refer to the king promised to the Jews.) Jesus is to be no military Messiah but a lowly sufferer. As someone has said, employing a musical metaphor, he transposed the messianic theme into a minor key. As another has put it, he also transposed it into a higher key, for the Christ is not merely a great man, as the Pharisees taught, but the Son of God. This is dramatically emphasized on the transfiguration mountain, where the power of the kingdom is displayed in the glory of its King.

On the mountain God reproves their failure to listen (9:7;

cf. 8:32f.), while at its foot Jesus rebukes their lack of faith. On the road to Jerusalem the gulf in outlook between him and his men becomes starkly and disturbingly clear and this puts his uniqueness into relief. He has called them to repent and believe (1:14), to follow him (1:17; 2:14), to deny themselves and take the cross as they follow (8:34). Now he speaks constantly of his coming sufferings and death while their thoughts are controlled by pride (9:34; 10:28), prejudice (9:38), presumption (10:13), and self-seeking (10:35ff., 41).

The reiterated cries of Bartimaeus and of the Palm Sunday crowds remind us that a king, David's greater son, is coming to Jerusalem, David's city. He has, however, already delineated the true pattern of authority in terms of service and the mode of his entry dramatizes this. Military kingship would have taken the horse for its symbol, not the donkey. For contemporary Judaism, the role of the Messiah is largely seen in terms of judgement on the other nations, but by word (the fig tree is an Old Testament symbol for Israel) and deed (the cleansing of the Temple) he declares God's displeasure with Israel herself.

He has come to religious Judaism's geographical centre. Now, towards the end of chapter 11, we see its religious leaders crowding into the Temple with the clear intention of discrediting him before the people. Every question put that day either by them or by him has direct or indirect relevance to the meaning of his person. What authority does he have? That of a beloved son. How does he relate to earlier revelation, to John the Baptist and the prophets? He is the summit of all revelation, the final messenger (12:6). What is his attitude to secular authority (Caesar), to Old Testament religious authority ('Which commandment is the first?'). At the end he focuses everything on the true nature of the Messiah. He is not just Son of David but Lord of all.

The Temple's beauty, greatly enhanced by the Herods, cannot conceal the religious leaders' ugly rejection of God's Christ, and it will be destroyed. Its judgement will anticipate the return of the messianic Son of Man, whose kingdom takes the place of the troubled kingdoms of men, whose order replaces the religious and natural instability of the present age, and whose words will endure when even the present form of the universe will dissolve.

It is clear then that the King will ultimately triumph. But what is the way to that glorious end? This he has emphasized time and again. It is the way of suffering and death. Chapters 14 and 15 present the facts about his closing hours. There is plenty of Old Testament quotation and allusion. God's purpose of atonement (10:45; 14:24) and vindication (8:31 – 'rise again'; 9:9, 31; 10:34; 13:26; 14:25, 28, 62) appears over against the malice of his enemies and the failure of his friends. The result is a story shot through with irony. An unknown woman (14:3–9) and an unknown man (14:12–16) serve him before he is taken and two men, new to the story, do so in the closing scenes (15:21, 43), while an intimate disciple betrays him, another denies him, and they all leave him. He has come into the world for the very purpose of dying, yet his enemies send to arrest him a band of men armed to the teeth. Except with his close disciples he has kept 'the messianic secret' of his person (1:34; 3:11; 9:9) but now he reveals it when it seems most absurd, for he is apparently a helpless prisoner in his enemies' hands (14:61f.).

Pilate's question about his kingship is probably highly sceptical. The Jews are under the Roman heel and hate it and yet they hand over to the Romans their rightful King. By mocking word and deed Roman and Jew call him king and saviour, which are in fact his rightful titles. The gospel of Mark was written originally for Roman readers. The Romans had devised crucifixion and used it to execute only those they most despised. On his cross Jesus asks in agony why God has forsaken him. Yet it is in such a setting that the very centurion in command of the crucifixion party confesses him to be Son of God!

So he is dead (note the emphasis in the last few verses of chapter 15), and the tomb is shut. But the gospel contains sixteen chapters, not just fifteen! The promise of resurrection is gloriously fulfilled and at the end of the book Mark shows us – as Luke has also done at his gospel's end and as the Acts of the Apostles begins – his ascent to the kingly place of universal Lordship (cf. 12:35–37; 14:62). So he is supremely relevant for all subsequent history, and his gospel is sent out to the ends of the earth with that message, while he provides living evidence of his own unconquered and unconquerable life.

Matthew

Matthew's account of the facts follows the same general pattern as Mark, but adds a lot of detail. It is very clear that Matthew wrote with Jewish readers especially in mind. This explains why his gospel was the favourite one in the early church when there were more Jewish in proportion to Gentile Christians than there have ever been since. To prove your right to kingship (as also to priesthood), your family tree was all-important, so Matthew starts by giving us the genealogy of Jesus. The Jews wanted to be sure someone who claimed to be the Christ really did match up to the Old Testament prophecies, and so he gives us a great many of these, especially in his first four chapters. These chapters might well make a deep impression on a Jewish reader with any degree of open-mindedness.

Then comes the great sermon on the mount. Jews suspected that Christians did not really take the Old Testament Law seriously. This sermon shows clearly that Jesus took it more seriously than anybody else had ever done. He showed its demands to be extremely far-reaching. The Jews of New Testament days were born into a culture where the teacher was highly regarded. This is not surprising as their religion and their culture can neither be separated nor understood apart. A book – the Old Testament – was in fact the basis of their whole way of life.

As the gospel goes on, we begin to realize that its author has given us much more of the teaching of Jesus than Mark, much of it cast in the culturally familiar form of the parable. Matthew was a tax-collector (9:9). This sort of job calls for gifts of organization and a 'pigeon-hole' mind, especially in those working for such able organizers as the Romans. We expect then to find the gospel material well ordered, and we are not disappointed. In fact, Jesus' teaching is largely to be found in five special sections, each concluding with the words 'when Jesus had finished these sayings' (7:28).

Because there is so much teaching and many an additional event recorded, this gospel is half as long again as Mark, but even so it can be read through in less than two hours. Read it to deepen the impression of its central character you have already gained from Mark. Chapters 26 and 27 present the closing events of his life in fuller form than in any of the other gospels and form the basis for Bach's *St. Matthew Passion*, often reckoned the greatest piece of music ever written.

Luke

Matthew wrote for Jews. However he belonged, like all the early Christians, to a church which had burst the confines of Judaism, and was going out in eager mission to the whole world. So his gospel ended with the great commission of Christ to eleven Jews to take the good news to every nation. Luke, himself a Gentile (that is, a non-Jew) and a member of Paul's evangelistic team, wrote especially for his fellow Greeks. If we are going to become Bible students we must enter imaginatively into the fascinating biblical world, and get the feel of it. Luke certainly helps his reader to do this. After a formal introduction in classical style, he takes them straight into the almost Old Testament atmosphere of the family circle of Jesus. At the start of chapter 2, the wider world is glimpsed as the backcloth to the nativity scenes. It comes more fully into view at the opening of the third chapter.

The Greeks were fascinated by *homo sapiens*. It was a Greek who said, 'Man is the measure of all things.' Here then is a man indeed, fulfilling all the ideals not simply of the Greeks, but even of God himself (3:22; 9:35). When Luke gives his family tree, he does not link him just with David, the father of the Messiah's tribe in Judah, and Abraham, the father of the

Jewish race, but with Adam, the first human being. The gospels
are not really quite like modern biographies. Their purpose is
to tell the good news of Jesus, not to record all the main events
of his life. Mark gives only the last three and a half years of
that life, with a third of his material devoted to the last week.
In this way we 'get the message' that his sufferings, death
and resurrection are of supreme importance for the good news.
Luke too concentrates on the climax of the story, but he is more
like a biographer than any of the other evangelists. For instance,
no other gospel writer tells us that Jesus was thirty when his
ministry started (3:23). Another human touch is to be found
in the frequent references to prayer (3:21; 5:16; 6:12 etc.): only
a dependent, fully human being prays. However, we have not
understood the significance of Jesus at all if we think of him
only as a quite exceptional man. The angel told the shepherds
that he was 'Christ the Lord'. That title 'Lord' was used by
Greek-speaking Jews to translate the great personal name of
God (Jehovah, better rendered 'Yahweh'). Luke uses this over
and over again in his narrative in application to this man, Jesus
(7:13; 10:1, etc.). The implication of this is quite clear.

In reading this gospel, look out for the name 'Jerusalem'
whenever it occurs. Luke uses it as frequently as the other three
evangelists combined, and in this way focuses our attention on
this city as the great place of destiny for Jesus.

John

The gospel of John is a literary marvel. Its vocabulary is so
small and its style so simple that quite a newcomer to the study
of Greek finds to his delight that he can make some sense of
it. But its simple language enshrines the deepest of truths. Those
who have read C. S. Lewis' *Narnia* books as children and
enjoyed them greatly as stories have sometimes returned later
to discover much deeper meaning in them. The gospel of John
is like that – although more, much more so – and it is not
fiction!

This book presents us with the same Jesus as the other three, but its approach is different in some ways. The first three gospels are often known collectively as the synoptics, because this word of Greek origin means 'seeing together'. What then are the differences between them and John? The titles we have found in the other gospels are all here, for 'Christ', 'Son of Man', 'Son of God' and many another may be discovered in the first chapter, as well as later in the book. Here too are miracles and plenty of teaching, and this story also ends with a cross and an empty tomb. Here too we are sure the man we are seeing is real flesh and blood like ourselves, for he is tired (4:6), is deeply moved, even to tears (11:33, 35, 38), and is gripped by an awful thirst in the midst of Calvary's agonies (19:28). Not only so, but there are plenty of familiar stories and sayings, although John gives us less common and more new material than the others, especially from Jesus' Judaean ministry.

We still have not answered the question. What is the real difference? Most of all, it lies in the development of certain profound themes which are found already in the synoptic gospels. The term 'Son of God' is used in all the gospels. Indeed, there are passages in the synoptics where its glorious content is spelt out for us (especially in Matthew 11:25–30 and Luke 10:21). We cannot examine John's record of Jesus' teaching on this theme in detail at this stage, but a glance at any one of several chapters in John (chapters 5, 8, 10, 14 or 17) will open a doorway into eternity and the very nature of God. Here then is teaching given to the intimate disciples which does not so much go beyond his teaching in the other gospels as expound it and bring out its implications.

John has in fact whetted the appetite of his reader by his mighty prologue (1:1–18). The first chapter contains many familiar titles for Jesus, but here is an unfamiliar one. He is the Word – the Logos of God. The reader may be a Jew to whom the Word of the Lord is God creating (cf. Genesis 1 and Psalm 33) and revealing, or he may be a Gentile who is used to the philosopher's use of this term to designate the real, inner, divine meaning of things. Both would expect to find in this book the disclosure of ultimate truth. They are brought up through its chapters to the cross where they see 'truth ... on the scaffold', and then to the upper room where, with Thomas, they fall at the feet of the crucified yet living Christ and cry in faith, 'My Lord and my God!' (20:28). You too?

2

JESUS IN THE BIBLE
Pondering the Facts

The line between presenting and reflecting on facts is not an easy one to draw, as anybody called as a witness in a court of law quickly realizes. Our presentation is influenced by our reflection even if this amounts only to selecting some items as important enough to present while others are omitted as less significant. The records of the life of Jesus are called 'gospels' because they tell the good news about him, and so even they present facts with meaning. This does not mean they are unreliable – far from it. An historian will seek to present his data accurately even though he cannot avoid interpreting them. Christians believe that God's Spirit worked with those who were in any case reliable witnesses so that their records present *his* truth and meaning, and not simply their own.

Peter

It is natural we should turn to the Acts of the Apostles after looking into the gospels. In the first ten chapters we read five sermons by Peter (in chapters 2–5 and 10). Here is the first preaching of the gospel after the gospel facts had been fully spelt out for us in the life, death, resurrection and ascension of Christ. The sermon in Acts 10, preached to a Roman centurion and his friends, is remarkably like an abbreviated form of the gospel of Mark. It is no surprise then to learn that an ancient and reliable tradition makes it clear that Mark wrote his gospel on the basis of Peter's memories of Jesus. It is interesting too to find a Roman centurion getting converted

towards the end of that gospel. The other sermons of Peter
were all addressed to Jews.

It is quite true that both at Pentecost and to Cornelius and
his friends Peter began with the *man* Jesus. Of course he did!
It all started for him when he responded to the call of a man,
and so it is with a man he starts his proclamation. But he goes
on much further. Jesus was a wonderful man of God. That
is clear in all five sermons. But there are special words and
phrases he uses which suggest he was much more. He was the
prophet foretold by Moses (Acts 3:22), the holy and righteous
one, God's servant (Acts 3:13, 26; 4:27, 30). In fact, he is both
the Saviour and the Judge of men (Acts 5:31; 10:42f.), and
it is clear that Peter believed their eternal destiny depended
on their attitude to this Jesus (Acts 4:11f.). No wonder, for
he was not only the Christ of God but Lord of all (Acts
2:36; 10:36).

Ever since quite early times, some readers of Acts have tried
to interpret Peter's statements about Jesus in a way that does
not tally with belief in the true deity of Jesus. They have laid
stress on expressions like 'God has made him both Lord and
Christ' (Acts 2:36) and 'God exalted him at his right hand as
Leader and Saviour' (Acts 5:31). Such statements have been
taken to mean that Jesus was at first simply a human being,
but that, as a result of his outstanding obedience to God, he
was exalted to a very high place indeed, so that men could treat
him as if he were virtually God.

Such 'adoptionism' rears its head from time to time. The
simplest way to answer it is to draw attention to the context
of such sayings. Remember that the first four of these sermons
were addressed to Jews in the very city where Jesus had been
crucified. It was essential that the greatness of their sin in
crucifying him should be brought home to them, so that, in
facing this sin in repentance, they might know the wonderful
grace of God. So Peter stresses that God has reversed men's
estimate of Jesus. 'You crucified ... and killed (him) by the
hands of lawless men, but God raised him up. . . . God has made
him both Lord and Christ, this Jesus whom you crucified.'

(Acts 2:23f., 36.) There is no new status in view here, but a contrast between man's rejection of him and God's warm approval. In Peter's final sermon, his audience is different and he makes it clear to his Gentile hearers that Jesus is the eternal Lord of all. There is no question of any 'adoption' into the Godhead. What could such an idea really mean anyway?

When people were converted to Christ they needed to be taught more about him. Much of this teaching was oral, but the New Testament contains many letters in which further instruction is given, related always to local needs. The two letters of Peter build on the basis laid in his sermons. Peter had spoken of Jesus as a wonderful man of God. He had lived with him for three years and seen his great beauty of character. There is a meditation on that character in 1 Peter 2:21–25. Peter's personal knowledge of him is its basis, but his language is coloured by the phraseology of Isaiah 53. He had also declared in his preaching that Jesus has a special place in the relations between God and human beings. This too he expounds in his letters. It is through Christ we have faith in God (1 Peter 1:21), through him our spiritual sacrifices are acceptable to God (1 Peter 4:11), through him we are saved from sin (2 Peter 2:20). The very highest claims are made for his master. He is Saviour and Lord. Even 'God' is not too great a word to apply to him (2 Peter 1:1).

James

As James Denney demonstrated many years ago in his book *Jesus and the Gospel*, every New Testament writer held basically the same view of Jesus of Nazareth. Their terminology varied, there were differences of writing style, even their emphasis presents some diversity. They all present him as truly human, but also as fully divine.

What about a book like the epistle of James? At first sight it seems to contain little that is relevant to our theme. Examine it more closely, however, and you will find that it has a Christology (that is, a way of understanding the significance of Jesus the Christ) as exalted as any in the New Testament. The letter is full of echoes of our Lord's ethical teaching, which he clearly considered authoritative (e.g. compare James 1:22ff. with Matthew 7:24–27). He is simply his slave, while he links his master (who was also his brother!) with God himself, and calls him 'Lord', the very 'Lord of glory' (James 1:1; 2:1). It is worth recalling that 'glory' was virtually a description of God himself in some Old Testament passages (e.g. 1 Samuel 4:21f.).

Paul

Saul of Tarsus was absolutely revolutionized in his life and thought by his encounter with the risen Christ on the Damascus road. There is a most interesting difference of perspective between him and the earlier apostles. People like Peter and John thought of Jesus Christ as the wonderful man who had called them from their fishing boats and whom they had followed for more than three years. How wonderful that he should now be seated at the right hand of God and acknowledged as Lord! Their master was now in heaven, so evidently divine. Paul's first encounter with him (as far as we know) was as the risen Lord. For him therefore the wonder was that this great divine one who had called for and captured his absolute allegiance had once lived a humble life of service on earth. Jesus was both man and God, but the perspective was different.

Paul makes use of some great titles and applies them to Jesus. He calls him 'Son of God' (e.g. in Galatians 4:4; Romans 1:4; 8:29 cf. Ephesians 1:5). He uses this title very sparingly; in fact, on average there are less than two examples per letter. To him it is a very exalted expression, and it has been pointed out that Paul's style always seems to become somewhat elevated in passages where the phrase occurs.

Does Paul ever actually call him 'God'? There are a number of passages where he seems to do so, although in some cases there are translation problems. A good case, however, can be made out for the translation of Romans 9:5 as 'who is over all, God blessed for ever.' In Titus 2:13 also Paul certainly appears to be calling Jesus God as well as Saviour.

Paul's favourite word for designating Jesus as divine is undoubtedly 'Lord'. He uses this word more than two hundred times and in the great majority of cases he applies it to Jesus Christ. As we shall see later, this title undoubtedly had divine meaning for the Jews and, therefore, for the earliest Christians. Especially important is Paul's expression *Maranatha*, which he uses in 1 Corinthians 16:22. This is composed of two Aramaic words, which should be rendered either 'Our Lord comes' or (more likely) 'Our Lord, come!' Some scholars have argued that Paul's doctrine of the deity of Jesus was taken over from Hellenism, with its belief in divine beings in human form. This just will not do. The Aramaic language of this phrase clearly indicates a Palestinian origin for it. Here then we have evidence of the faith that Jesus is Lord as found among Palestinian Jews, who had been reared as strict monotheists.

If Paul can use such great terms of Jesus, it is not surprising that in Colossians 1:15–17 (cf. 1 Corinthians 8:6), he should say that he is the great Creator and Sustainer of the whole universe. Paul sees him as Lord over all, for 'firstborn of all creation' is reminiscent of the place of special privilege and authority in the family held by the firstborn in Old Testament times (cf. also Psalm 89:27). Even great spiritual beings exist only because of his activity and indeed with a view to his glory, for everything was created for him as well as by him. Colossians 1:17 presents us with a fact of great philosophical importance. This vast and almost infinitely diverse universe is only maintained in its ordered being by his constant activity. No wonder this same epistle speaks of him as the incarnation of the very 'fullness of deity' (Colossians 1:19; 2:9).

Genesis 1–3 must have come gloriously alive with new meaning for Paul as a result of his conversion. Not only did he see God the Creator in terms of Christ, but he believed Jesus to be the new head of the human race, as Adam was its original head. He is the truly representative man, the last Adam (Romans 5:12ff.; 1 Corinthians 15:45–47). Paul speaks the same language here as in the Acts of the Apostles. Luke records a

Pauline sermon delivered at Athens, and in this he spoke of
the two great significant men, even though Adam is not actually
named in the presence of a Gentile audience to whom he would
mean nothing (Acts 17:26, 31). As the last Adam Jesus is the
image and glory of God (2 Corinthians 4:4; Romans 8:28–30).

We shall need to look very carefully at Philippians 2:5–11
at a later stage. In some respects this is the most comprehen-
sive statement about Christ contained in the New Testament.
Paul dwells especially on the humiliation which the incarnation
involved for Christ, and on the exaltation to the place of supreme
power and authority which followed the deepest point of his
humiliation, his shameful death on the Roman gibbet.

The writer to the Hebrews

The letter to the Hebrews is anonymous. It was ascribed to
Paul fairly early but not early enough to make sure it is by
him and weighty objections have been advanced against this
ascription. It is best to treat it as a separate entity. It is chiefly
concerned with the work of Christ and with its superiority to
the Old Testament order of things in every sphere. We can
never really understand that work, however, unless we grasp
the fact that it takes its value from his person. The one who
offered the great final sacrifice was both God and man. The
writer therefore starts his letter with a great four-verse statement
of his deity.

Jesus is the last word of God to men, not just in his speech
but in his person. He can be this because he is the exact
representation of all that God is in his inmost nature, the
Creator and Sustainer of all that exists, and because he has
dealt finally with sin and occupies the place of supreme power.
For reasons that relate to the special problems faced by the
first readers of his letter he goes on to demonstrate the absolute
uniqueness of Jesus over against other spiritual beings, the
angels who played such a big part in the earlier and fragmentary
revelation given in Old Testament days. He quotes a number
of Old Testament passages in support of his thesis. Some of

these are conventional messianic passages, but others bear particularly clear testimony to his belief that Jesus is God incarnate, for, in their Old Testament setting, they apply not to the Messiah but to God himself. This is a most striking fact.

Hebrews chapter 2 presents the complementary truth of the humanity of Jesus, and the writer shows how important it is that he should enter fully into the human situation. He is the Saviour of men and he could not really do this work at all without full identification with those he came to save. There are other passages in the letter which dwell on the humanity of the Saviour, none perhaps more moving than a short passage in chapter 5 (verses 7–10). The reference to 'loud cries and tears' makes us realize that his prayer-life was not play-acting but a real cry for strength from above in the face of the most awful pressure from temptation and suffering. Only as he came this way and learned in testing what obedience really involved could he come to that perfection of experience which was the human complement of his eternal divine fitness to be our Saviour. The writer undoubtedly considered his true humanity to be of quite special importance, for, as a study of the Greek text reveals, he gives unusual emphasis to the human name Jesus almost everywhere it occurs.

John

The Johannine group of writings makes many important contributions to New Testament Christology. The fourth gospel is no less a Jewish book than the gospel of Matthew, even though John emphasizes so much the universal relevance of Jesus Christ. Here we see Jews eagerly awaiting the fulfilment of God's promise of a Messiah (John 1:41, 45, 49; cf. 20:30f.). Here too, as in the synoptic gospels the terms 'Son of Man' and 'Son of God' are applied to him. There is no doubt though, that John lays special stress upon his relationship to God as his unique Son. He is God's 'only-begotten Son' (1:14, 18; 3:16, 18; cf. 1 John 4:9). An interesting, but little-known fact is that John never applies the term 'sons of God' to Christians (some

English versions are a little misleading in this respect), but always refers to them as 'children of God'. Take the two facts together, and you cannot escape the conviction that John held the relationship of Jesus to God to be absolutely unique, without any parallel in other human beings.

Some aspects of the teaching of the fourth gospel were mentioned in the previous chapter. The other Johannine books also make their contribution to our theme. These books relate particularly to the spiritual needs of the church at Ephesus and other churches in the area. Ephesus was an important centre for the teaching of Greek philosophy. Ever since man began to ponder the meaning of the universe and his own place within it, he has been fascinated by a number of great basic questions. What is life? What is truth? What is love? John knows the answer to questions like these. One answer may be given to them all, not in terms of philosophical definition but in terms of God incarnate. God is the source of all values and so when God became incarnate in Christ, life, truth, love, and many other abstract ideas came into concrete manifestation (1 John 1:1; 4:8–10, 16; 5:11; cf. John 1:4; 5:26ff.; 11:25).

The book of the Revelation is unique in the New Testament and even in the Johannine group. It consists of a series of visions and the imagery it uses is drawn very largely from the Old Testament. In this book, Jesus is presented as the Lamb of God in the midst of the throne of God (Revelation 5:6). This phrase is applied to him a great many times but in each case we ought to remember this first occurrence of it. The Lamb has suffered and yet is triumphant. His victory has been achieved at great cost to himself.

John has no doubt as to the true manhood of Jesus, for he appears in a vision to him as 'one like a son of man' (1:13). A study of this passage alongside Daniel 7, where this phrase first occurs, reveals something most striking. The picture of the risen Christ in Revelation 1 combines characteristics of the Son of Man and of the Ancient of Days (God) as these are displayed in the Old Testament chapter! Could John have shown us any more clearly his belief in the unqualified deity of this Jesus?

Coming as it does right at the start of the book, this vision sets the tone for all that is to follow. We are not surprised then to find that each of the letters to the seven churches (in chapters 2 and 3) commences with a series of great titles of the Lord Jesus, some of them with clear overtones of deity. At its end, he calls himself 'The Alpha and the Omega, the first and the last, the beginning and the end.' Such language has already been applied to God in the book (1:8), and in any case would remind the Jewish reader of similar language used of the Divine Being in the pages of the Old Testament (Isaiah 44:6; 48:12). Jesus Christ is Lord and God.

3

JESUS IN THE BIBLE
Predicting the Facts

The risen Lord Jesus Christ met two of his disciples on the road from Jerusalem to Emmaus. They did not at first know him, but he used the Old Testament Scriptures and showed himself to them in its various books. Later the same day, he did virtually the same for the whole group of his disciples (Luke 24:25–27, 44–46). How does Christ meet us in the pages of the Old Testament?

He does so in a number of different ways. We meet him in *pictures*. The New Testament writers use terms like 'prophet', 'priest' and 'king' of him. These terms suggest pictures; they come from the Old Testament, because there we have legislation and other information which enables us to see the kind of functions these men were called by God to perform. There is also an imperfect picture of him presented in the lives of godly men in the Old Testament. He alone is perfect, but just as we portray Christ in so far as, by his grace, we live to his glory, so did those who lived in Old Testament days. Such pictures are called 'types', and Christ as the great fulfilment of them all is the 'Antitype'.

Christ is also viewed in *prediction*. The Old Testament looks beyond itself to a future day when God will reveal himself in some new and special way. Ezekiel, for example, declared the judgement of God on the shepherds (the kings and other leaders) of Israel. God then promises, 'Behold, I, I myself will search for my sheep, and will seek them out.' (Ezekiel 34:11). The Lord Jesus fulfilled this. He and the New Testament writers often use shepherd language about him (e.g. in John 10 and 1 Peter

2:25; 5:4); and he also said, 'The Son of Man came to seek and to save the lost' (Luke 19:10). So he is God revealing himself, but he is also God's great man of the future, for there are many passages in Old Testament books which look forward to a great king, a perfect prophet, an eternal priest, and which find their fulfilment in him.

The Old Testament also furnishes a preparation for him in its *phraseology*. New Testament terms like 'wisdom' (e.g. 1 Corinthians 1:24) and 'word' (e.g. John 1:1, 14) need a literary setting to give them fullness of meaning, and the Old Testament (e.g. Proverbs 8 and Psalm 33) provides this. In other words, such language comes into the New Testament from the Old, heavily laden with Old Testament meaning, and gives still more clarity to what the New Testament writers claim for Christ and what he claimed for himself.

Does he ever appear in the Old Testament in *person*? There is some evidence to suggest that he does. There are passages which refer to the Angel of the Lord and where it seems that an ordinary created angel is not in view, for the Angel speaks as if he is God and yet in some way as if he is distinct from him. Such a phenomenon would be well explained if these appearances were seen to be pre-incarnate manifestations of Christ. We shall start our more detailed study of Christ in the Old Testament with this Angel.

The Angel of the Lord

Hagar, Sarah's maid and the mother of Ishmael, was found by the Angel of the Lord beside a spring of water in the wilderness. He spoke to her, not in the name of God but as if he were God. The story comes to its conclusion with the words, 'So she called the name of the LORD who spoke to her, "Thou art a God of seeing"; for she said, "Have I really seen God and remained alive after seeing him?"' (Genesis 16:13). His appearances may also be studied in passages like Genesis 22, Exodus 3 and 14, Judges 13 and Zechariah 3. Genesis 18 and 19 are also illuminating. Study these chapters and you will notice that although three men came to Abraham he spoke to one only. It is said, without explanation, that the Lord spoke to him, that the men left for Sodom but Abraham still stood before the Lord (Genesis 18:22), and finally that *two* angels arrived in Sodom (Genesis 19:1). It may well have been the same person who confronted Joshua as the captain of the Lord's host (Joshua 5:13–6:2) and who wrestled with Jacob (Genesis 32:24–30; cf. Genesis 48:15f.; Hosea 12:3–5).

It is, of course, one thing to say that this is a divine person, but something more specific to assert that he is none other than a pre-incarnate manifestation of Christ. Can we take this further step? On general grounds, we certainly can. If, as the New Testament shows us, Christ is the great revealer of God, then we would expect to see his activity in this kind of phenomenon. If he is not Christ then who can he possibly be? The Spirit of God inspires the word of God but there is no instance of his personal appearance in human or angelic form.

Can we find any grounds for such an identification within the Old Testament itself? We could establish the matter if we could find clear links between the Angel of the Lord and messianic prophecy, that is, prophecy which finds its focus in the man of the future and which is fulfilled in Christ. There are three such possible links. The name of the Angel of the Lord is 'wonderful' (Judges 13:18) and so is the name of the messianic King (Isaiah 9:6). Moreover, this word is normally used in reference to deity. If Malachi 3:1–4 speaks of the Messiah, and if 'the messenger of the covenant' in verse 1 stands in apposition to 'the Lord of hosts', then we have additional evidence. Finally Micah 5:2, which identifies Bethlehem as the birthplace of the messianic King, also indicates that he had a life long before he was born there, and perhaps, that he had some involvement in ancient history.

It should be said, of course, that such pre-incarnate manifestations anticipate but are not real parallels to the incarnation. The latter was a unique fact because only in Jesus of Nazareth did God actually come in a real human life from the womb to the tomb.

The perfect prophet

The prophet occupies a very important place in the Old Testament. It is not easy to say when prophecy began. Some tend to think of it as starting with Samuel, or Elijah, or even Amos. Yet the writer of Psalm 105 clearly believed that the patriarchs were in some sense prophets of God (verse 15). A prophet was the mouthpiece of God, and so it is not surprising to find that Moses is regarded as the supreme prophet.

In Deuteronomy 18 the use of soothsayers, diviners, and others who claimed special knowledge of and power over the unseen world is condemned. Then comes a passage in which Moses promises that the Lord would raise up for the people a prophet such as he. This is followed by a condemnation of false prophecy. In one sense we may see the fulfilment of this promise in the long line of prophets to be found within the history of the nation of Israel, but the Book of Deuteronomy itself suggests that this is not the whole story. In its closing chapter the death of Moses is recorded. When this chapter was written we do not really know, but the writer was sure that the promise of chapter 18 had not been perfectly fulfilled by his day. These are the closing lines of Deuteronomy:

> There has not arisen a prophet since in Israel like Moses, whom the LORD knew face to face, none like him for all the signs and the wonders which the LORD sent him to do in the land of Egypt, to Pharaoh and to all his servants and to all his land, and for all the mighty power and all the great and terrible deeds which Moses wrought in the sight of all Israel.

There seems to have been a lively expectation of the fulfilment of this promise at the time of Jesus. The priests and Levites asked John the Baptist, 'Are you the prophet?' (John 1:21). The people recognized Jesus as a prophet (Matthew 21:11). The feeding of the five thousand brought an immediate reaction from the crowd. 'When the people saw the sign which he had done, they said, "This is indeed the prophet who is to come into the world!"' (John 6:14.) This thought may have been stimulated in them by the miracle for, they would think, here was the new Moses giving new manna from heaven (cf. John 6:30–35).

The New Testament preaching included the assertion that Jesus fulfils this prophecy (Acts 3:22–24). In one respect, however, he went far beyond any prophetic ministry to be found in the Old Testament. It was chiefly in his words that a prophet made known the truth of God. No doubt qualities of godliness in them provided illustration of the truth they proclaimed, although this was not always the case. Balaam and Hosea represent two extremes here. In the case of Jesus, however, lip and life were completely in harmony, so much so that John can speak of him as the Word of God made flesh (John 1:1–18). Here the revelation of God comes in the total event of Christ, not simply in his verbal utterances. This is what the writer to the Hebrews means when he says that God has now spoken in a Son (Hebrews 1:1f.). Hebrews 1 contains no reference to the teaching given by Jesus but concentrates on his person and his activities in creation and redemption. It is in the full fact of Christ that God is heard and seen.

The perfect priest

The prophet represented God to the people, while the priest represented the people to God. These two functions have been well described as descending and ascending mediation respectively. In the book of Genesis it was the head of the family who acted as its priest, building altars and offering sacrifices. Under the Mosaic legal system, however, the tribe of Levi was set apart for duties connected with Israel's place of worship, and within this tribe the clan of Aaron was selected for priestly functions. At the apex of the whole system stood the high priest. One day in the year, the Day of Atonement, was a very special one in the life of the people (Leviticus 16). On this day, the high priest acted as the representative of the whole people. Only on this day could the most sacred part of the tabernacle (or, later, the Temple) be entered, and then by him alone. Bringing with him sacrificial blood, he pushed aside the great curtain that shut off the Holy of Holies, and entered it on behalf of the whole people.

The priests of Israel were very concerned to preserve their genealogies, for they needed to be able to demonstrate their pedigree to be able to function as priests at all. It would not seem possible therefore for Jesus to be a priest, because he was a member of the tribe of Judah. He needed to be of Judean blood if he was to fulfil the functions of king. In this way, the powers of the king and the priest were for ever separated within the normative Old Testament structure. Yet one New Testament writer fastens upon an interesting exception to the rule within the Old Testament itself and argues for the true high-priesthood of Jesus on the basis of it. The writer to the Hebrews points to Melchizedek (Hebrews 5:6, 10; 6:20–7:19). He appears in the Genesis narrative (Genesis 14) without any genealogy, because of course he belongs to the pre-Mosaic period, and yet he was clearly recognized by Abraham, a man of God and the most eminent ancestor of the nation, as a true priest. Here then is the biblical precedent for a non-Aaronic priest.

The writer to the Hebrews could in fact make out a very strong case. He quotes several times from Psalm 110 and here, in a messianic psalm, the psalmist writes, 'You are a priest for ever after the order of Melchizedek.' This means that the significance of Melchizedek had not been missed by the psalmist himself, so that prediction and not just history supports the validity of the priesthood of Jesus. He stands for us, he offered himself as the great sacrifice for us, and now intercedes for us before the throne of God.

The perfect king

Deuteronomy looks forward to the prophet like Moses. It also anticipates the kingdom and provides a constitution for the king (Deuteronomy 17:14–20). This constitution is not, as in modern western monarchies, imposed from below, but rather it is imposed from above: it is God-given. It emphasizes that the king must be an Israelite, must be pure in devotion to the Lord, must not regard military might as the foundation of his kingdom (the horse was, of course, employed in warfare), nor seek riches. He should be a humble man of God who seeks to order his personal life and his kingdom in accordance with the written law of God.

Did any monarch fulfil this ideal? Not perfectly, but David with all his faults approximated more nearly to it than most. He therefore becomes a kind of standard for kingship in the Old Testament. The books of Kings constantly evaluate the reign of a king of Judah in terms of his conformity or lack of conformity to the example of David (1 Kings 11:38; 15:3, 11 *et al.*). In fact, Judah's tribe (Genesis 49:10) and David's family (2 Sam. 7) provide the continuing line of valid monarchs for God's people, up to the division of the kingdom for the people as a whole, after it for the southern kingdom, which the Old Testament simply calls Judah.

2 Samuel 7 is a foundational chapter for the hope of a continuing line of kings, and of course the messianic hope is built on this. It is clear that Solomon is specifically in view in some parts of this chapter, for he was the offspring of David and built the house of God. He is called 'son of David' with great frequency in the Old Testament. But if you compare the record of his life and reign with the constitution given in Deuteronomy 17, you will see clearly that he fell short of this ideal most strikingly. This means that the Old Testament contains within itself evidence that the promise of a great 'son of David' was not fulfilled in Solomon and that we must look beyond him.

In psalm after psalm we see the great messianic king behind and towering above the historical king (e.g. in Psalms 2, 45 and 72). Isaiah fills in a great deal of detail for us (Isaiah 7:10–18; 9:6f; 11:1–10 and 32:1–8), and other prophets too have much to contribute. The number of passages relevant to the theme is so vast that we cannot survey it adequately in the space available. The picture that emerges is one that must have been most attractive to the Jewish reader. The throne had been occupied by such a wide variety of men, all of them imperfect and some extremely wicked and oppressive. Isaiah had himself known five kings. With what delight must he have received the revelation of a king who would reign supreme but whose reign would be a blessing not only to his own nation but to the whole world, including even the animal kingdom (Isaiah 11), and who would be absolutely just in all his dealings with his subjects!

The perfect servant

The book of Isaiah provides us also with another very important line of preparation for the coming of Christ. Biblical scholars have long recognized that certain passages in it can be taken together and that they form a series dealing with the theme of God's Servant. They are known as the Servant Songs. These are Isaiah 42:1–9; 49:1–13; 50:4–9 and 52:13–53:12 (accepted by virtually all scholars although there is still some difference of opinion as to the length of the first two), plus Isaiah 61:1–4, which is accepted by many as part of the series, and even Isaiah 63:1–6 which has been suggested as a final Song.

Prophets, priests and kings were all servants of God, and the nation of Israel herself was called to be his servant. At first, we are not sure whether the servant that appears here is to be thought of as an individual or whether he is a personification of Israel or some group, perhaps the godly remnant, within the nation. As however we move from one Servant Song to another, we become increasingly aware of the fact that the language, however applicable in part to a group, seems to be contemplating an individual, whose dedication to God's service is complete and who suffers greatly in fulfilling God's design for his life. In some ways he seems to sum up in himself elements of the three great offices of prophet, priest and king. Like a prophet he speaks for God (Isaiah 49:1; 61:1ff), like a priest he is engaged in the offering of sacrifice (Isaiah 53:10), like a king he wins victories and divides spoil (Isaiah 53:12) and is exalted to a place of great authority (Isaiah 52:13).

The Jews were themselves uncertain whether a group or an individual was intended in the Songs. Those who thought in terms of an individual were themselves quite unsure as to his identity. In fact, many of the godly characters of the later part of Old Testament history and also of the inter-testamental period were suggested at one time or another. It cannot be said that modern biblical scholarship has reached any greater consensus. What concerns us, however, is how the Songs are interpreted within the Bible itself. There is interesting language suggesting a partial fulfilment in Jeremiah 11:19 ('I was like a gentle lamb led to the slaughter;' cf. Isaiah 53:7), but for all his faithful service to the Lord and his suffering as a result of that faithfulness, there is language in these Songs that goes far beyond Jeremiah. The New Testament writers of course apply them to Christ, and there is evidence within his own teaching that he believed himself called to fulfil the destiny depicted in these passages. See, for example, the quotations from Isaiah 53:12 in Luke 22:37.

The righteous man

The story of Israel embraces the lives and activities of a great number of men and women. Among them are characters of true godliness. Not one is perfect, but men like Abraham, Joshua, Moses, David and many another show clearly that they loved the Lord and wanted to serve him and to bring glory to his name. All godly character points to the Lord Jesus Christ. This is true for the Christian, but it is also true of the men of the old order. When we read their story in the full light of the New Testament, we can see much in them that reminds us of him. In a way, even their sins point to him, because they show by their imperfections the need for the coming of him who is perfect.

This Old Testament literature not only presents us with many an insight into the characters of these imperfectly godly men but it does something more. It presents us with ideals of godliness. Take Psalm 1, for example. This may have been written specially to open the psalter, although we cannot be sure of this. It shows us piety and ungodliness in contrast, and of course depicts the godly life in ideal terms. Such an ideal stood upon the pages of Holy Scripture for the rest of Old Testament history and throughout the inter-testamental period. It no doubt furnished a challenge and a stimulus to godliness – but it was never perfectly exemplified. Then Jesus came, and the ideal took flesh.

The son of man

A few passages of Scripture have been given names which are chiefly employed in theological circles. One of these is Genesis 3:15, which has been known for a long time as the *protevangelium*. This Latin word, meaning 'the first gospel', fastens on the element of promise contained in what, strictly speaking, is a curse on the serpent. It is the promise that he will be overcome by a human being, the 'seed of the woman'.

An expression often used as a synonym for 'man' is 'son of man'. 'What is man that thou art mindful of him, and the son of man that thou dost care for him?' (Psalm 8:4; cf. Numbers 23:9). A study of the historical development of biblical words and phrases is fascinating, for a word that begins quite simply will often come to its ultimate meaning filled to the brim with profound truth. That certainly happened with the phrase *the son of man*. It is used by God when he is addressing Ezekiel and is employed in his book so frequently that you can probably find it by opening the prophecy at random. Why? God is revealed to this prophet in all his majesty and holiness, and the use of this phrase, suggesting as it does the human frailty of the recipient of the revelation, may be intended to underline the divine greatness still more. Having been used to address one prophet, however, we discover that it is used in this way again, this time in Daniel 8:17. We begin to see, then, that it is coming to have something of a technical sense, and now seems to be a natural phrase to use of a prophet, and perhaps could be employed of other servants of God.

Psalm 80 represents perhaps a further step. Here Israel is depicted in the figure of a vine. In verse 15 the people are described collectively as 'this vine, the stock which thy right hand planted'. In verse 17 the figure changes. Now the psalmist cries out, 'Let thy hand be upon the man of thy right hand, the son of man whom thou hast made strong for thyself!' Another synonym for man? Yes, but much more. The man, or son of man, here would seem on the face of it to be Israel. The rabbis however had a most interesting interpretation of this verse. The Targum (an Aramaic paraphrase of an Old Testament passage, which certainly reflects rabbinic theology) on these words, translates 'son of man' as 'king messiah'. Perhaps then, as the rabbis thought, verse 17 does not simply apply to Israel but to the king who summed up the nation in himself. Even if their interpretation is incorrect, it at least shows that the title could be applied to a king as well as to a prophet.

All this prepares us for the supreme passage, Daniel 7. Daniel is given a vision of four great beasts rising up from the sea one after the other. Then there is a judgement scene presided over by the 'one that was ancient of days' (i.e. Almighty God). The beasts are judged, but then, apparently in a separate but related vision (Daniel 7:13ff.), the prophet sees 'one like a son of man' who came, not from the sea but with the clouds of heaven, and who received a kingdom which was universal and, unlike the kingdoms of the beasts, eternal.

Who is this 'son of man'? The four beasts symbolize both four kings (verse 17) and also the kingdoms they rule and represent (verse 23). Although the language of verses 13 and 14 is applied specifically to a group ('the saints of the Most High', verses 18, 22), the analogy of the beasts would suggest that the son of man too is an individual and not simply a group. He is a king, but is not viewed simply in himself but as the head of a community.

The 'son of man' in Daniel 7 fascinated some non-biblical Jewish writers, like the man who composed a document called *The Similitudes of Enoch*, but our chief interest in it lies in the fact that Jesus applied it to himself. It was in fact the self-designation which is found on his lips most frequently in the synoptic gospels and occurs too in the fourth gospel. So it suggests real humanity, but also kingship and even heavenly origin.

The son of God

The phrase 'son of God' does not occur with great frequency in the Old Testament. We find it being used of angels, but always in the plural (Job 1:6; 2:1; 38:7 and, possibly, Genesis 6:2). The fact that it is never applied to them in its singular form justifies an otherwise puzzling statement from the writer to the Hebrews (Hebrews 1:5). Sonship and likeness are ideas which belong very much to each other in Hebrew thought, and so the angels may be called 'sons of God' because they are like him in being spiritual beings – although other theories have been advanced to explain the terminology.

More important for our purposes is the use of the phrase in application to Israel. In Exodus 4:22f. God appeals to Pharaoh as one father to another: 'Let my son go that he may serve me; if you refuse to let him go, behold, I will slay your first-born son.' God takes up this people Israel, adopts them (cf. Romans 9:4), and lavishes on them all the love and care a father gives his son – and more, because he is God and not man. So Hosea pictures God as the tender father holding out his arms to the little son as he makes his first attempts at walking (Hosea 11:1).

As the term *son of God* has been used with reference to the nation as a whole we are not surprised to find it applied to them in its plural form (Deuteronomy 14:1; Isaiah 1:2). Once again, however, we find no use of it in the singular to designate an individual, with the important exception of the king. He is called 'son of God' in three passages. 2 Samuel 7:14 is the basic one, because both Psalm 2:7 and Psalm 89:27 assume the certainty of the promises in 2 Samuel 7 and so are founded on them. Each of the three are passages where we find ourselves compelled to think not simply in terms of an historical king but also of the great messianic King. It is a term applicable to the king because he sums up the chosen nation and because he foreshadows the great King of the future. Yet we need to say that whatever it was in certain forms of paganism, it was hardly a mere synonym for 'king' in the Old Testament. Had it been this we might have expected it to be used more generally. It is a term of relationship rather than one of office, and this relationship was seen in all its fullness, indeed in a unique form, when Jesus of Nazareth came into our world as *the* Son of God. It was this relationship that fitted him for the kingly office *par excellence*.

4

HISTORY AND FAITH

Henry Ford is supposed to have said 'history is bunk!' Is this sentiment right? Much has been written about the period in which we are living. It has been called 'the affluent age' (despite economic pressures and the fact that the third world is still anything but affluent) and 'the permissive age'. Another marked quality of it which is very important for our subject is its lack of interest in history. Sir Winston Churchill reckoned that it was the study of history, even more than philosophy and economics, which was vital for a politician. It has been well said that the nation that has not learned from its history may have to repeat it. On the other hand, there is truth in the somewhat cynical comment that the one thing we learn from history is that we learn nothing from history.

The Bible and history

What has all this to do with our theme? A very great deal. Christ came in history. When Luke introduced the story of his birth, he set him in his historical ('Caesar Augustus', 'Quirinius') and geographical ('Syria', 'Nazareth', 'Judea', 'Bethlehem') context (Luke 2:1–4). We have four gospels and each of them lays great emphasis on events.

Not only so, but the gospel writers clearly believed they were narrating the most important events ever to have happened in the world. The opening of Luke's third chapter is particularly significant from this point of view:

In the fifteenth year of the reign of Tiberius Caesar, Pontius Pilate being governor of Judea, and Herod being tetrarch of Galilee, and his brother Philip tetrarch of the region of Ituraea and Trachonitis, and Lysanias tetrarch of Abilene, in the high-priesthood of Annas and Caiaphas, the word of God came to John the son of Zechariah in the wilderness.

Luke gathered together an impressive list of names of eminent people, including the most important political figure in the known world. But he was really drawing attention *away* from them all to a tiny scrap of desert in a remote province. John mattered more than all the others, because he was the herald of the Christ. The others simply represented the stage setting for the action of vital importance.

Christianity is based on history, the history of the man Christ Jesus. But the story of Christ comes to us in the context of a book of history. Almost everywhere you look in the Bible you are confronted with history. The books of the Old Testament, from Genesis to Esther, are all historical in form, and even those that have a large legal content are set in an historical framework. Some of the psalms survey a period of Israel's history, and the prophets all pronounce God's word in relation to the history of their own period.

There is history in the New Testament also after the gospels. Acts gives us the story of the first generation of church history, and the epistles contain many reminders that they emerged from that history and were written to real groups and individuals with their own place in the story. The last book of the Bible presents an awesome picture of the Lord Jesus Christ enthroned as supreme over the world's history and destiny.

It is as well then that we should think about the connexion between our faith in Christ and the historical events upon which it is based.

The background of the Old Testament

Does it matter that the Lord Jesus Christ came as the climax of a long historical story? Does it matter that he was born into the nation of Israel, and that people like Abraham, Jacob, Moses, David and many another belonged to that story?

Yes, it does indeed, and for a number of important reasons.

The Old Testament give us a lot of really basic truth about God, truth given by him to his people. It was in the course of the history of the people of Israel that they were taught this truth. They learned through his dealings with Abraham and Moses that he was a God who makes and keeps covenants. They learned through the events of the Exodus that he is a God of mercy and judgement. They learned through his dealings with them in the land over many years that he is a God of great patience and long-suffering. All these lessons, and countless others, were stamped on their minds and hearts in relation to historical events, as these events were interpreted to them by the men of God he sent to do that very thing. All these truths, and the history upon which they are based, are important, because it was *that* God, and no other, who became man in the Lord Jesus Christ.

Then the Old Testament is important because it gives 'body' to many of the terms used by the New Testament in connexion with Christ. Terms like 'prophet', 'priest', 'king', and so on are meaningful in terms of many cultures, but their exact meaning in application to Christ must be learned from the Old Testament background. We could easily misunderstand them unless we looked into Old Testament teaching and history for their meaning. This is even more important with terms like 'Son of God', 'Lord' and 'Saviour', which were being employed in the Graeco-Roman world in New Testament times. We must understand them in terms of the Jewish background of belief in one holy God and not the Graeco-Roman world with its polytheism and its failure to link religion and morality.

So this Old Testament background gives marvellously full intellectual content to the great words and phrases applied to the Lord Jesus Christ in the pages of the New Testament. Faith is essentially trust in a person, but it cannot exist unless we have an idea as to who that person is and what he is like. The more we learn of him, so the richer faith becomes on its mental side, and the greater its formative influence upon our lives can be.

A further value of this historical background lies in the fact that the Old Testament, both in itself and in its relationship to the New, shows us how absolutely trustworthy God is, how true to his word of promise, so that we are encouraged to make a wholehearted commitment to his final word, the Lord Jesus Christ himself. There are plenty of examples of God's faithfulness in the Old Testament. God gave Abraham great promises. He said that he would make a great nation of his seed and give him a land in which this nation would live (Genesis 12:1ff., *et al.*). He kept these promises. Isaac's descendants did become a great nation and they were given the land of promise.

Christ is himself the supreme example of the trustworthiness of God. The promises of God in Old Testament times seem like a number of streams flowing independently. As we have already seen, the people of Israel were encouraged to look forward to a number of great figures. The New Testament proclaims that in one person all these figures are united. As Paul puts it (2 Corinthians 1:20), 'All the promises of God find their Yes in him.'

Spend time reading the Old Testament. Seek to understand what it meant for the people to whom it was written, but look also for Christ in its pages, and learn from it that God is to be trusted when he makes promises, is to be obeyed when he issues commands and is to be feared when he gives warnings.

The gospel narratives

It is impossible to exaggerate the place of the gospels in the Bible. Many Christians make the mistake of concentrating on the epistles without giving enough attention to the gospels. 'Rabbi' Duncan, a great Christian scholar of an earlier generation in Scotland, said towards the end of his life that if he had his life over again he would give some of the time he had spent on the epistles to deeper study of the gospels. Now we cannot spend too much time on the epistles, but neither can we on the gospels, and the latter really form the necessary basis for the former.

The gospels record facts, they record history, they tell us about events, conduct, teaching, miracles, deeds of love, acts of judgement, sayings of wisdom – in short they spell out what kind of person the Lord Jesus Christ really was. They arose almost certainly out of a great need for facts amongst the early Christians. The apostles were dying one by one. Soon the church would be bereft of those who had first-hand access to the things that had actually happened in the life and ministry of the Lord Jesus. They needed a permanent record, backed by authentic apostolic witness. This became theirs, and is now ours, as the four gospels were written.

Faith grows as it feeds on facts, not on feelings nor on fancies. Faith is greedy for facts; it has an insatiable appetite for them. John tells us that the whole purpose of his gospel is that faith might be created and might grow.

> Now Jesus did many other signs in the presence of the disciples, which are not written in this book; but these are written that you may believe that Jesus is the Christ, the Son of God, and that believing you may have life in his name.

This statement (John 20:30f.), although written specifically about one gospel, is surely true of them all. The early preachers, and every Christian preacher since, preached Christ, but 'Christ' is a mere word without content unless we tell people who he was and is, what he has done and what he can be to them. The gospels have an enormous part to play in this.

A study of the New Testament as a whole reveals that there is one basic gospel which forms the background to it all. There have been attempts to disprove this, but the case against it is not easy to make out. Paul really sums up this gospel in 1 Corinthians 15:3f. when he says:

> For I delivered to you as of first importance what I also received, that Christ died for our sins in accordance with the scriptures, that he was buried, that he was raised on the third day in accordance with the scriptures.

The gospels are rightly so called because in fact they reflect this gospel and fill out its details. They tell us who the Christ was, and they spend much of their space preparing us for his death and resurrection and recording the events themselves.

Also in the gospels we find Christ calling men to faith. It was after the disciples had been with him for some time and had observed his life and listened to his teaching that they confessed him to be the Christ (Matthew 16:13ff.). It was through their actual contact with the facts that the divine revelation came. The gospels still do that kind of work today when people approach them with a willingness to learn and an openness to receive truth through them.

Acts to Revelation

The Acts of the Apostles is a book of vital importance. It is the only historical record we have of the first generation of the church's life. It is therefore highly informative and interesting. It is however more than that. Luke's two volumes are intimately related to each other. There are all sorts of points of contact between them, and fascinating and spiritually profitable comparisons between the life of Christ and the life of the church can be made from a study of the two taken together.

As he opens his second volume, Luke gives Theophilus a brief reminder of the contents of volume one. In it he had dealt with 'all that Jesus began to do and teach'. That word 'began', coupled with many a reference later in his second book, makes us aware of the fact that Acts should be thought of as the record of what Jesus continued to do and teach – from his throne in heaven and through the Holy Spirit. It was the exalted Christ who gave the Holy Spirit (Acts 2:33), and it was in the name of Jesus that the church did what she did (Acts 3:6, 16; 4:30, *et al.*). At various points the risen Christ appeared as a reminder that he was at work (Acts 7:55; 9:3ff.; 9:10ff.; *et al.*). So the book encourages faith in Christ, in the contemporary Christ, the Christ of faith who is also the Jesus of history. Churches as well as individual Christians need to grow in faith, and the Acts of the Apostles is a major means of grace for local churches.

The *epistles* are certainly well designed to strengthen faith.

They take the historical basis of the faith for granted and they interpret the historical, crucified and exalted Jesus in a wide variety of ways. Each letter has its characteristic emphasis, its function in showing us something further of the Lord Jesus. His example of godly and innocent suffering is given to us in 1 Peter, the deep meaning of his death and resurrection is brought out in Romans, his exaltation is the subject of much teaching in Ephesians, his supremacy over every kind of being in Colossians, his superiority to everything provided in the Old Testament order in Hebrews, and so on. For a full understanding of the many-sidedness (and yet essential simplicity) of the Christian gospel, which reflects the fullness of Christ himself, we need to read every book of the New Testament. We cannot afford to neglect even the shortest of them if we would know him in fullest measure.

The book of *Revelation* is unique in the New Testament. There are a number of passages (e.g. Mark 13) and even books (e.g. 1 and 2 Thessalonians) which have much to say about Jesus' second advent (second coming). Here, however, is the one long book which has his return as its main subject. We might well say that even this book is historically orientated, provided we can use a phrase like 'future history' without contradiction.

The book professes to deal with facts which, although not part of history when they were written, were, the writer was convinced, as sure to be as if they already existed. But there are two important ways in which it is very much anchored in past history. First, it is written to seven churches in the Roman province of Asia, actual local churches set up during the kind of evangelistic enterprises of which Acts tells us. Secondly, its main theme is the activity in judgement of the Lord Jesus Christ from the throne in heaven, and the term used over and over again to describe him is 'the Lamb'. Now this phrase, symbolic as it undoubtedly is, nevertheless points us to history. It is a sacrificial term. The New Testament uses this kind of language about the cross, so that 'the Lamb' is the crucified Christ, who also rose from the grave. We have the evidence of the gospels to underline these historical facts for us.

The Jesus of history and the Christ of faith

For a century and more there has been a great deal of debate about the relationship between Jesus as he really was and what the Christian church believes him to be. This debate has gone through a series of stages. It is not the function of this book to take up questions like this, nor would there be the space to do it justice.

What can and needs to be said, however, is that although the fundamental historical documents of the Christian faith are 'gospels', and so are really a kind of preaching, they contain a great deal of evidence to support their general trustworthiness. We have already thought of the problems raised by the difficulty of harmonizing the accounts of the resurrection, and have seen that this testifies for rather than against their truthfulness. Perhaps one more illustration might be given. In Mark 13:32, Jesus is speaking of his second advent, and he says, 'But of that day or that hour no one knows, not even the angels in heaven, nor the Son, but only the Father.' Now some have doubted if he ever used the term 'Son of God' in reference to his person. Yet here it is in a saying which has caused difficulty to Christians ever since it was written! We shall look at its implications in a later chapter, but it is quite inconceivable any Christian should have invented it. It is in the gospel because Christ said it – and it includes a reference to his divine sonship.

5

FROM HEAVEN TO EARTH

Our space age has got used to the idea of a universe 'out there' and to the possibility of exploring it from earth. Is it this place 'out there' the Bible means by 'heaven'? Not really. The Jews used to speak about three heavens. Nearest to us is the first, where the birds fly. Next comes the second, where the sun and the moon and the stars are. Last of all is the home of God. Now the big difference between the first two and the third is that they are visible while it is not. This is the main distinction the New Testament makes. There is a visible and there is an invisible universe and it is this invisible realm to which chiefly the name 'heaven' is given (Colossians 1:16). The Lord Jesus spoke about coming down from heaven in order to give life to the world (John 6:33, 51). What then does the Bible teach us about his life before he came at Bethlehem?

He was always with God

In the fourth century there was a serious heresy called Arianism, which has reappeared in different disguises in more recent times. The Arians were prepared to say all sorts of high-sounding things about Jesus Christ, but they stopped short at the most important point. They were not prepared to say that he was God. The greatest man who had ever lived? – Yes! The greatest being in the created universe? – Yes! God? – No! So, they said, 'there was a time when he was not.'

This is not what the Bible teaches. John declares, 'In the beginning was the Word, and the Word was with God, and the

Word was God. He was in the beginning with God.' (John 1:1f.) This great passage really makes four statements about him. The third of them is of supreme importance and we shall look at it later. Notice for the moment, though, that the fourth is a combination of the first two, and so has the effect of emphasizing the point John is making. Our English word 'with' here is a translation of a very common Greek preposition. However, it is rather uncommon in this particular sense. Its basic meaning is 'towards'. This suggests then that John is saying not simply that Jesus the Word was always with the Father but also that he was, in a sense, facing towards him, so that they were for ever in fellowship with each other. John goes on at the end of his prologue to speak of Christ as the one who was 'in the bosom of the Father' (John 1:18). This again implies close fellowship.

In his teaching in the gospel of John the Lord Jesus often used language which suggested that he had a kind of 'home-sickness' for heaven (John 8:23; 13:3; 14:28; 16:28). It is particularly interesting to be able to listen in to his prayer, as he addresses the Father shortly before the crucifixion (John 17). This prayer reflects a beautiful intimacy of love and shows that this relationship existed before the universe came into being (John 17:24). He speaks also of the glory he had with the Father before the creation (John 17:5).

It is not only in the gospel of John that this kind of teaching occurs. Paul, for instance, when writing to the Corinthians and seeking to stimulate them in their Christian giving, uses – as he so often does – the highest possible illustration: 'For you know the grace of our Lord Jesus Christ, that though he was rich, yet for your sake he became poor, so that by his poverty you might become rich.' (2 Corinthians 8:9.) When was Christ rich? We can search the gospels from end to end without discovering any wealthy period during his earthly life. In earthly terms he was anything but rich. This expression then can only have meaning if we relate it to his life before he came into the world, his eternal life with God.

He created everything

Modern man has a bigger conception of the universe than any have had before him. Modern science is still discovering how vast it is, and presents statistics to us that baffle our minds and that our faculty of imagination cannot really handle. If we take the Bible's teaching seriously, every new discovery will serve only to make us more aware of the supreme greatness of Christ, who created it all.

For this is indeed what the Bible teaches us about him. Let us return to John 1. We have already considered the first two verses. The third reads, 'All things were made through him, and without him was not anything made that was made.' Paul takes up this theme in two passages particularly. In 1 Corinthians 8:6 he states, 'For us there is one God, the Father, from whom are all things and for whom we exist, and one Lord, Jesus Christ, through whom are all things and through whom we exist.' In Colossians he spells this out in a little more detail when he says, 'In him all things were created, in heaven and on earth, visible and invisible, whether thrones or dominions or principalities or authorities – all things were created through him and for him. He is before all things.' (Colossians 1:16f.) Finally, the writer to the Hebrews, writing of the Son of God, says of him, 'through whom also [God] created the world.' (Hebrews 1:2).

This teaching is simply staggering. He was born as a baby, probably six or seven pounds in weight, nineteen or twenty inches long, and yet he was the Creator of everything that is! Why do our New Testament writers say that the universe was created 'through him'? Because they believed in the Father as well as the Son ... One of the many things John is suggesting when he uses the term 'Word' of Jesus (John 1:1, 14) is that we should interpret Genesis 1 with its oft repeated 'and God said' in terms of Christ. It was God's Word that created the universe, but that Word was not simply a meaningful sound but a person. He made everything through his eternal Son.

He sustains everything

Creation is an act or a series of acts. It is of course a manifestation of great power, revealing that the Creator is almighty. Just as wonderful, however, is the power to keep in being what has been created. This too is ascribed to Christ. After writing of his creative work, Paul goes on to say, 'and in him all things hold together.' (Colossians 1:17.) The scientist marvels at the order of the universe and the artist sees beauty in that order. All these things are held together in their ordered structure by the Son of God. This thought provides the Christian student with a standpoint from which to view ordered structure in his own chosen field of study. All true order comes from his Saviour, for he is also the Creator and Sustainer of everything that exists.

The writer to the Hebrews takes this thought even further in two ways. He says that Christ upholds all things by his word of power (Hebrews 1:3). This suggests that we are not to think simply in terms of impersonal laws. What we call law in the universe is simply evidence that God is consistent. Everything began with the uttered word of God (Genesis 1), and it continues in its ordered being on the same basis. The picture of Atlas in Greek mythology shows us a man carrying the universe on his shoulders. This is not a proper parallel to what the New Testament says of Christ. The word translated 'upholding' really implies motion. It suggests either a universe in motion – which would, of course, fit marvellously into the scientific model of the universe – or that Christ himself is moving, perhaps carrying everything forward in accordance with a plan. It may even suggest both.

He rules everything

This takes us a little further still. When we think of the universe apart from personal beings like men and angels, it is enough to say that Christ upholds and sustains it all by his power. The idea of a kingdom, however, suggests personal beings who are called to submit to his will and serve his purposes. Paul speaks of Christ as 'the head of all rule and authority' (Colossians 2:10). The terms he uses here probably refer to spiritual beings, angels of great power, good or evil. If they apply to them, however, how much more true must it be that he rules over every human authority!'

It is worth remembering that if Jesus is both God and man, he now reigns in virtue of both facts. It is the right of God to rule. If he cannot rule, then who can? We shall see later that the New Testament also relates Christ's right to rule everything and everybody to his true humanity and to his work of redemption.

In the gospel of John, there is an important change at the close of chapter 12. Up to this point, Jesus has been working and teaching openly amongst the Jews. In chapters 13–17 he takes his close disciples aside and concentrates upon them. Chapter 12:35–50 brings his ministry among the Jews to a close and John comments upon it, partly in the words of Jesus himself, but also, in verses 36b to 43, in his own words. He uses two quotations from the book of Isaiah, the first from chapter 53 and the second from chapter 6. Then he makes this astonishing statement: 'Isaiah said this because he saw his glory and spoke of him.' (John 12:41). Now it is no surprise to us that he believed Jesus is to be seen in Isaiah 53, because we could find a dozen New Testament passages which imply the same thing. What is so startling is the thought that in the Temple in Isaiah 6 the prophet saw the glory of Christ. Isaiah 6 is one of the most awe-inspiring visions of the Old Testament. The seraphim acknowledged the utter holiness of the Lord, the prophet abased himself and confessed his sinfulness and the Lord spoke his word of great authority. He is 'the King, the LORD of hosts' (Isaiah 6:5). So the Son of God, long before he came to earth and before his exaltation to a kingly throne as man, reigned over everything from heaven as God.

He revealed God

If, as we saw in chapter 3, the Son of God manifested himself from time to time in the world as the Angel of the Lord, then here is evidence that he was revealing God in Old Testament times. Does this mean then that he was one of those who revealed God to the men of Old Testament times, or can we go further than this and say that, in some sense, all revelation of God at this stage was really revelation through him? If Isaiah 6 is a revelation of him, how many other parts of the Old Testament could be also?

We may get some light on this matter from Peter in his first letter. He writes about the Old Testament prophets (1 Peter 1:10–12), and says:

> The prophets who prophesied of the grace that was to be yours searched and inquired about this salvation; they inquired what person or time was indicated by the Spirit of Christ within them when predicting the sufferings of Christ and the subsequent glory. It was revealed to them that they were serving not themselves but you, in the things which have now been announced to you by those who preached the good news to you through the Holy Spirit sent from heaven, things into which angels long to look.

This passage links together the word of God in the Old Testament and in the New, and attributes both to the Spirit of God. It would be no surprise to us if Peter used the term 'Spirit of Christ' about the New Testament revelation, because he assured his hearers in Acts that the Holy Spirit sent from heaven came from the risen Christ (Acts 2:32f.). What is most significant is the fact that the Spirit of God in his work in the Old Testament prophets is called by this title. It seems that the Holy Spirit in his work of imparting divine truth to and through men worked in both testaments as the divine agent of the divine Christ.

If this is the case, then we can now read John 1:1–18 in an even deeper way. Jesus is the Word of God, not only because he brought the fullness of revelation from God when he came in the flesh, but because all true revelation of God, long before the incarnation, was not only revelation of him, having him as its great subject, but revelation through him. He is the master-revealer who instructs everyone through whom God's truth comes to men.

He is God

We have left this point to the end. It hardly needs to be proved now, because all the other leading statements in this chapter point in this direction. If he created everything, sustains and rules everything and is the one great revealer, how can we stop short of saying that he is God? No wonder John goes on from the statement 'the Word was with God' to assert 'and the Word was God'. (John 1:1.) The omission of the definite article in the Greek before 'God' does not have the significance that some sects have tried to give it. It does not and cannot mean that the Word was 'a god', for what could such a statement mean to a Jew (and John was a Jew) but that he was a pagan deity? No, the omission of the article here is a perfectly regular way in Greek to show that 'the Word' and not 'God' is the subject of the clause. It also emphasizes the divine nature of the Word. The gospel which opens in this way comes to its climax in the worship of Jesus by Thomas, when he declares, 'My Lord and my God!' (John 20:28.)

6

THE UNIQUENESS OF JESUS

'No man is an island.' What I do concerns my neighbour and what he does affects me. We have all been deeply influenced by many other people, especially those who are particularly close to us as relatives or friends or teachers, but also by many we have never met. We have encountered some of these through books or television. One of the features of our modern world is the extent to which many of us are influenced by contemporaries who are quite unknown to us in personal contact.

As we grow up, 'hero-worship' plays an important part in our life. Young people today tend to get 'sold' on a pop-star, who occupies the centre of attention for some months or for a year or two, and who is then often replaced by another. During the period of his influence he makes an impact upon his devotees at various levels. They listen to his music, they try hard to get to see him, they may be influenced by him in their dress and in other aspects of their life-style. It is when the moral features of life begin to take the colour of the 'idol' that the effect of this kind of 'worship' becomes really serious. Such a position of influence is an immense responsibility.

What then of the influence of Christ? There can be no doubt that he makes a most profound impact on those who come to know him and that he does so especially at the level of character. There can be no question of mere 'hero-worship' as far as he is concerned. He demands our full devotion as the Son of God and as Lord of all. There cannot be any question of moving from him to somebody else. The person who thinks that allegiance to Christ can be tried out, as if it were a kind of experiment, has not begun to understand his claims and demands, or what the gospel is really all about. Coming to him is the decisive beginning of a lifetime's commitment to one who claims to be our Lord and God.

The Bible teaches us that he is alive today, and this is the basis of his living influence upon us. It is not simply a question of following the life-style of somebody from the past but of the effect of fellowship with a wonderful living person now. Yet the New Testament teaching about his character does matter. If he was like that then he is also like it now, for 'Jesus Christ is the same yesterday and today and for ever' (Hebrews 13:8). In this chapter we are going to look at the Bible's teaching about his character.

His awareness of no sin in himself

We begin with the gospels. Here we see a life of great beauty. The closer a man or woman is to God the more sensitive he or she becomes to sin, yet Christ showed no consciousness whatever of personal sin. Just the opposite! He said to the Jews, 'Which of you convicts me of sin?' (John 8:46.) The Bible recognizes Satan as the spiritual power at work in sinful men (e.g. in Ephesians 2:1–3), but Jesus said, speaking of Satan, 'The ruler of this world is coming. He has no power over me; but I do as the Father has commanded me, so that the world may know that I love the Father.' (John 14:30f.)

John the Baptist was sent to baptize those who had turned from their sins in response to his preaching (Matthew 3:1–10). Then a new baptismal candidate presented himself, Jesus of Nazareth. John immediately recognized that such a baptism was not appropriate for Jesus, and did not want to perform it. It was at this point that Jesus said, 'Let it be so now; for thus it is fitting for us to fulfil all righteousness.' (Matthew 3:15.) Whatever this saying means, it certainly shows us very clearly that he was not coming because of personal sin. If he had been aware of any fault, this would have been the moment to say so.

Rather he saw the baptism as a fulfilment of righteousness, the working out of God's plan for his life.

It is often when a man is aware of the imminent end of his life that he finds he has to face his moral failure and admit it to himself. In the case of our Lord, the exact opposite is true. At one stage in his ministry, he was speaking about God, and he declared, 'I always do what is pleasing to him.' This sense of perfect fulfilment of God's will lasted him right to the end, for it was only just before the crucifixion that he said, 'I glorified thee on earth, having accomplished the work which thou gavest me to do.' (John 17:4.)

The testimony of others

But can we really take these claims seriously? Surely such unconsciousness of sin might be the product of delusion, not of real goodness! In theory, yes, but this cannot be true in the case of Jesus. His own awareness of being without sin finds plenty of confirmation. Those who were closely involved in the events that brought him to his trial and to the cross confessed that he was innocent of the charges brought against him (Matthew 27:4, 24; Luke 23:47). An evil spirit, no doubt unwillingly, went much further than this, and declared that he was the Holy One of God (Mark 1:24).

The New Testament writers accepted the fact of his sinlessness without any question at all. Peter had known him intimately and walked the dusty streets of Palestine with him for three years and more. His verdict (1 Peter 2:22f.) was this:

> He committed no sin; no guile was found on his lips. When he was reviled, he did not revile in return; when he suffered, he did not threaten; but he trusted to him who judges justly.

John may well have been closer to him than anybody else during his ministry. Many years later, after a lifetime of pondering the facts, he wrote, 'You know that he appeared to take away sins, and in him there is no sin.' (1 John 3:5.) Paul was a violent persecutor of the Christians before he was converted to Christ on the Damascus Road. He says that he 'knew no sin' (2 Corinthians 5:21), and, later on in the same letter, he entreats his readers 'by the meekness and gentleness of Christ' (10:1).

Sinlessness may seem rather a negative quality. It is very clear however that the Lord Jesus did not maintain his freedom from sin by avoiding human contact and by living the life of a hermit. Peter sums it up so aptly and positively in a simple, direct statement, when he says 'he went about doing good' (Acts 10:38).

Most significant of all, however, is the verdict of God the Father himself. When God spoke in an audible voice in Old Testament days, it was to set out his moral demands on men, the Ten Commandments. When he spoke with an audible voice in New Testament days, it was to express his pleasure in his Son, who had fulfilled his commandments. At his baptism, God said, 'Thou art my beloved Son; with thee I am well pleased.' (Luke 3:22.) The silent years of his youth and young manhood had been pleasing to God and he was pleased with the baptism itself. Later on, after many months of ministry, God again declared his pleasure in him on the mount of transfiguration (Matthew 17:5).

The holiness he revealed

Holiness, in its basic meaning, is really distinctness. God is holy, for he is distinct from us and from his whole creation. For us to be holy is to be set apart for God and to live a life that is distinct in the sense that we are living it for God. The Lord Jesus certainly revealed that he was holy. The angel Gabriel told Mary, before Jesus' birth, 'The child to be born will be called holy, the Son of God.' (Luke 1:35.) Luke also gives us a glimpse into his childhood. The story shows us that Jesus had a thirst for God and for the things of God. It shows equally clearly that he accepted the role of an obedient son in his earthly family. 'And he went down with them and came to Nazareth, and was obedient to them.' (Luke 2:51.)

His holy resolve to do his Father's will was put to the test in the temptations he encountered in the wilderness, just after his baptism and prior to the start of his ministry. Matthew (4:1–11) and Luke (4:1–13) give us the details. At his baptism, God had declared him to be his Son. Twice Satan said to him, 'If you are the Son of God....' He was not so much trying to put a doubt in his mind about his divine Sonship, but rather to get him to presume on it. 'What is the use of being God's Son unless you use your privileges!' was really what he was saying.

Jesus replied to him each time in the words of Scripture, each passage taken from Deuteronomy 6–8, and so perhaps this was the passage he had himself been making the basis of his devotional meditations in that time of testing. This was God's word, and it was his word for him, because he was a true man. He was really reminding the devil that a son not only has privileges but also responsibilities. It is the place of a son to obey his father. So the temptations were resisted and the will of God for his life, a will that would involve suffering, was embraced. These temptations were absolutely real, as we shall see.

The tempter often returned to the attack in later months (John 6:15; Matthew 16:22f.), but the Saviour never yielded an inch to him. At last the time of his appointed sufferings drew near and his will to obey God again faced challenge in the garden of Gethsemane. His human nature shrank from the awful suffering involved in atonement for sin, but he did not follow natural inclination but the will of God. 'My Father, if it be possible, let this cup pass from me; nevertheless, not as I will, but as thou wilt.' (Matthew 26:39.)

In the sermon on the mount and elsewhere in the gospels we find Jesus setting out the ethic of the kingdom of God; but he was always the best illustration of his own teaching. He loved his enemies and prayed for those who persecuted him, he made no attempt to serve two masters but did only the will of his Father in heaven. His absolute dedication to that will stood out particularly clearly on the road to Jerusalem – as recorded for example in Mark 8:31–10:45 – in contrast to his disciples. They were seeking greatness and power for themselves (Mark 9:33ff.; 10:28, 35ff.). He was treading the path of humble service that led to death. He did not come to be served but to serve and to give his life a ransom for many (Mark 10:45).

The love he showed

Love takes us out of ourselves in self-giving to others. The whole life of our Lord was characterized by such an outlook. There are several references in the gospels to his great compassion for the needy crowds of people (e.g. Matthew 9:36; 15:32). This compassion drew him into contact with countless numbers of individuals who experienced his saving and healing power in so many ways. A study of these contacts shows us that he touched a cross-section of the people of Palestine in his day.

Luke in particular stresses that the love of Christ brought him into contact with those who were despised or under-valued by the society of his day. Lepers were excluded from ordinary society, but he not only cleansed them from their leprosy but even touched them, something no Pharisee would ever have dreamed of doing (Luke 5:12–14). Tax-collectors were regarded as beyond the pale because of their daily contact with Roman officialdom, but he not only ate with them and their despised friends, but actually called one of them to be a member of the inner band of his disciples (Luke 5:27–32). The Roman occupying force was hated, yet he healed the servant of a centurion and remarked upon the greatness of his faith (Luke 7:1–10). A great barrier of hatred had grown up between the Jews and the Samaritans. He rebuked two of his disciples because of their failure to love them (Luke 9:52–56). Women and children, the poor and the needy, were all the objects of his loving care and concern. Yet he also came to bless the rich and the respectable, so the story tells us that at the close of his life Joseph the rich man and Nicodemus the Pharisee showed him an answering love by preparing his broken body for the tomb (John 19:38–40).

We have already stated that he was the best illustration of his own teaching. He told his disciples that they were to love their enemies (Matthew 5:44–48):

Love your enemies and pray for those who persecute you, so that you
may be sons of your Father who is in heaven; for he makes his sun
rise on the evil and on the good, and sends rain on the just and on
the unjust.... You, therefore, must be perfect, as your heavenly
Father is perfect.

Such perfection was certainly shown in his own life. He wept
over Jerusalem and expressed his great longing to take its people
into his loving arms (Matthew 23:37–39; Luke 19:41–44), yet,
as he well knew, this city would be the scene of his crucifixion
in just a few days and its people would yell out for his blood.
The story of his last days contains many evil characters but
even amongst these Judas Iscariot stands out for his treachery,
deceit and ingratitude. Yet Jesus extended the hand of friend-
ship to him to the very end, handing him a tasty morsel at the
table in the way an honoured guest was treated (John 13:26f.),
and, in the very moment of the betrayal, addressed him as
'friend' (Matthew 26:49f.).

The wisdom he possessed

Wisdom is a moral quality. Knowledge increases with experience
and with education, but it is only as we have wisdom that we
can put that knowledge to proper use in daily life. For wisdom
to be truly moral it must be related to God's purpose and
the goals he sets before human beings. No man is really wise
unless he lives in the will and for the glory of God.

Jesus had a wisdom which was recognized by ordinary people.
He taught in the synagogue of his own home town, and the
people said, 'Where did this man get this wisdom and these
mighty works? Is not this the carpenter's son?' (Matthew 13:54f.)
He had great insight into character, as the stories of Nicodemus
and the woman of Samaria in chapters 3 and 4 of John's gospel
show us.

Perhaps the best study of his wisdom is to be found in the
record of the great day of questions (Mark 11:27–12:44). Just a
few days before his death he was teaching in the Temple at
Jerusalem. He was asked many questions. Some of these

questions were put by the religious authorities as such, others by various sectarian groups, while one at least was put by a private individual. To them all Jesus answered with amazing wisdom. He avoided the traps set for him by his enemies and turned their questions against them. Each answer too served the spiritual purposes which were so very important at that time. It was vital that people should recognize his authority (Mark 11:27–33) as the Son of God (Mark 12:1–12), whose ministry underlined the claim of God to man's obedience (12:13–17), who was soon to rise from the dead (12:18–27), and whose new way enabled men to love God and neighbour (12:28–34). At the end, he turned to them and asked them the most central and vital question of all. Who is the Messiah? Is he just a man or is he Lord of all (12:35–37)?

Wisdom is a quality which gives balance to character. What men call holiness can so often become harsh and what they call love can degenerate into sentimentality. There was neither in the character of Jesus. Holiness and love existed in him in perfect combination, in perfect balance. In fact, love existed in its highest and, we might well say, its only true form, because he always had a concern that men should be holy, so that all his actions towards them were motivated by that great concern. It is doubtful whether love that does not serve the ends of holiness deserves to be called by that name.

The standards he fulfilled

The standards of God for man's life are made clear and plain in his word. We gain our understanding of his will from the whole Bible of course, but there are particular passages which have always been recognized as summaries of what the godly life will involve in moral terms. Let us look at some of these and see how each finds its perfect fulfilment in the character of Jesus Christ.

The Decalogue, or the Ten Commandments, occupies a place of quite special importance in the Old Testament. God gave them to his people in awe-inspiring circumstances and in an audible voice (Exodus 20). They were written upon tablets of stone by the 'finger of God' and they are really the basis for the rest of the legislation given in the Old Testament. Every one of these commandments found complete fulfilment in the life of Jesus of Nazareth. His worship and service were directed towards the true God alone. Indeed, the fact that he kept the commandments is so obvious that detailed discussion of it would seem to border upon insult. It is worth noting, however, that the fourth commandment is no exception. Our Lord kept the sabbath day, but he rejected many of the applications of the sabbath legislation given by the Pharisees. He treated it as a gift of God to men ('the sabbath was made for man') and, over against the Pharisaic interpretations of it, set his claim to interpret and apply it as the Lord of the sabbath (Mark 2:27f.).

In the sermon on the mount he emphasized that outward conformity to the commandments was not enough, but that God searches the very motives of the heart (Matthew 5:21–30). God judges hatred and lust as well as murder and adultery. The Decalogue itself seems at first sight to be concerned mostly with outward acts. The tenth commandment, however, concentrates on the motive, because it declares, 'Thou shalt not covet!' It is interesting to notice that Paul, before he became a Christian, found that one particularly searching (Romans 7:7):

> If it had not been for the law, I should not have known sin. I should not have known what it is to covet if the law had not said, 'You shall not covet.'

So Jesus, in his teaching, was really extending this inward principle to other parts of the law. Take any of the commandments and search as deeply as possible into its implications for the motives, the inner springs of conduct, and you will find that Jesus presented perfection in his own life. For example, parents are to be honoured; so, while he was suffering the acute agonies of the cross, Jesus made loving provision for the future of his mother (John 19:25–27).

The sermon on the mount opens with a series of blessings, usually known as the Beatitudes (Matthew 5:3–11). There are many other beatitudes in the Bible. For instance, Psalm 119 opens with the words, 'Blessed are those whose way is blameless, who walk in the law of the LORD!' John heard a voice speaking from heaven and saying, 'Blessed are the dead who die in the Lord henceforth.' (Revelation 14:13.) Every beatitude of Scripture, except of course where it is related to the forgiveness of someone's sin (e.g. Psalm 32:1), finds its perfect fulfilment in him. Who else was, in an absolute sense, meek, merciful and pure in heart?

On one occasion, the question of the greatest commandments was raised. Both he and the questioner agreed that the command to love God with your whole being and to love your neighbour as yourself were the two greatest commandments of God (Mark 12:28–34). In his first letter, John shows us that the two cannot really be divided from each other (1 John 4:20f.):

> If any one says, 'I love God,' and hates his brother, he is a liar; for he who does not love his brother whom he has seen, cannot love God whom he has not seen. And this commandment we have from him, that he who loves God should love his brother also.

Now there is no doubt that the two were present to the absolute degree and in the most perfect combination in the character of Jesus Christ. He knew that the Father's will for him meant the cross, and his love for him caused him to embrace this, with all that he knew of its terrors, as the final step in the programme of his life. This was at the same time the ultimate proof of his great love for sinful men and women, because he came to die for them. John says, 'Having loved his own who were in the world, he loved them to the end.' (John 13:1.)

Paul, writing to the Galatian Christians, set out the basic qualities of the true Christian character in terms of the fruit of the Spirit. 'The fruit of the Spirit is love, joy, peace, patience, kindness, goodness, faithfulness, gentleness, self-control.' (Galations 5:22f.) Each of these was present in fullest measure in the Lord Jesus Christ. The first of them is, of course, the most basic of all, and Paul wrote one of his best-loved passages (1 Corinthians 13) on this theme. Read through this chapter. Does the character here depicted remind you of anybody in particular? It is surely a picture of Christ himself, the very incarnation of love. As an experiment, substitute your own name for the word 'love' (or 'charity' in the Authorized Version). Few experiments can be more searching or challenging. Now use the name of Christ there. His name fits perfectly wherever the word 'love' occurs in the chapter. It has been truly said that the fruits of the Spirit are the virtues of Christ.

7

THE COST OF IT ALL

Self-giving, especially when it takes a person through a deep valley of sorrow or suffering, is extremely moving for the onlooker. So much in this world is done with an eye for praise or for personal gain, that people are very impressed when they see a love that is pouring itself out at real cost to the one who loves. The life of Jesus Christ was like that, not only in its end, but throughout its whole course. There must have been an element of suffering in his human experience from the very beginning, and this element became more and more dominant as his life moved to its terrible climax.

The Servant Songs, which we considered briefly in chapter 3, show this note entering more and more into his experience. The first song (Isaiah 42) simply suggests that there would be factors in his ministry which would have made many another fail or be discouraged. The second (Isaiah 49) seems to view the ministry of Jesus in retrospect; so verse 4: 'But I said, "I have laboured in vain, I have spent my strength for nothing and vanity; yet surely my right is with the LORD, and my recompense with my God."' He is then described as 'one deeply despised, abhorred by the nations' (verse 7). Isaiah 50:6 shows the spite of his enemies beginning to take the form of physical violence. 'I gave my back to the smiters, and my cheeks to those who pulled out the beard; I hid not my face from shame and spitting.' It is in the fourth song (Isaiah 52:13–53:12) that the note of suffering comes to dominate the picture, and these sufferings culminate in death.

A later volume in this series is to deal with the work of Christ,

so that we shall not be considering the cross as a sacrifice for
sin, or, indeed, giving any thought to the work of Christ as
effecting salvation for us. It is, however, right in this volume for
us to think about his sufferings in relation to his person. What
did Calvary and all the sufferings and sorrows that preceded it
mean to him? We cannot understand this in any full way, but
can reverently follow up any light the Bible throws on the
subject. It should serve to deepen our sense of wonder and
gratitude.

His human feelings

The gospels are just full of language showing us that our Lord
posessed truly human emotions. Mark, in particular, uses a
number of words signifying strong feeling. He says that Jesus
was 'moved with pity' when a leper came for cleansing (Mark
1:41). Almost immediately, in verse 43, he uses another word
which is very difficult to translate, because it normally suggests
anger: 'And he sternly charged him, and sent him away at once,
and said to him, "See that you say nothing to any one."' This
anger may have been due to his knowlege that the man had
every intention of disobedience, as the account itself shows. The
main point for us, though, is that both are real human feelings.
In Mark 3:5, we read, 'And he looked around at them with
anger, grieved at their hardness of heart.'

We could go right through the gospel, illustrating this point,
and could add evidence from Matthew, Luke and John. We
shall simply note that the gospel writers sometimes refer to deep
sighing. When the Pharisees were seeking a sign from him, in
order to test him, 'he sighed deeply in his spirit' (Mark 8:12).
We know what it is to express distress or longing or disgust in
this inarticulate way. So did Jesus. No suggestion that his
sufferings were just play-acting and not real can possibly be
accepted. They do not stand in the gospels on their own, but
in the context of a true human experience in which emotion
played a real part.

His sinful environment

The Old Testament contains a number of moving passages which seem to be virtual cries from the heart of God. In Deuteronomy 5:29, God says, 'Oh that they had such a mind as this always, to fear me and to keep all my commandments, that it might go well with them and with their children for ever.' In Psalm 81:13f., he cries, 'O that my people would listen to me, that Israel would walk in my ways! I would soon subdue their enemies, and turn my hand against their foes.' The book of Hosea has much of this kind of language (Hosea 11:8f.):

> 'How can I give you up, O Ephraim! How can I hand you over, O Israel! How can I make you like Admah! How can I treat you like Zeboiim! My heart recoils within me, my compassion grows warm and tender. I will not execute my fierce anger, I will not again destroy Ephraim; for I am God and not man, the Holy One in your midst, and I will not come to destroy.'

This kind of language is found too in the gospels, although now on the lips of one who was not only divine but human. Jesus was deeply stirred by the unbelief of the people around him. Mark tells us that he marvelled at their unbelief (Mark 6:6). When he found failure of faith not just in the people generally but in his own disciples, he cried out, 'O faithless generation, how long am I to be with you? How long am I to bear with you?' (Mark 9:19.) The most poignant of all these sayings is to be found in his mournful cry over rebellious Jerusalem. 'O Jerusalem, Jerusalem, killing the prophets and stoning those who are sent to you! How often would I have gathered your children together as a hen gathers her brood under her wings, and you would not!' (Matthew 23:37). The repetition of the name of the city, the vivid illustration of parental concern taken from the animal world, and the contrasting uses of the word 'would', all serve to underline the deep concern that must have been in his heart at that time.

It is not easy for us to imagine what the presence of a sinful environment all around him must have meant to Jesus. He was holy, and he had come to earth from the realm where all was holy. Many a Christian has wept tears of anguish over men and women who would rather have the sin that destroys men than the Saviour who blesses them. What must the sinless Saviour himself have felt when he saw on every hand men and women failing to give glory and thanks to the God who had given them everything they ever possessed, and were determined to go their own way despite the eternal consequences?

His experience of hostility

Christ always divides men. The gospel writers show us two processes working at the same time. He was gathering disciples but his enemies also began to emerge (Mark 1:16–20; 2:13f.; 3:1–6, 13-19). The Pharisees and Herodians (Mark 3:6) were poles apart in their general outlook. The Pharisees held themselves aloof from the occupying Gentile forces, while the Herodians collaborated with them. But they became united by a powerful stimulus. They hated Jesus. The priestly Sadducees, too, came into this unholy alliance (Matthew 22:23–34).

John in his gospel, in chapter after chapter, shows Jesus in controversy with groups of Jews. The chief priests and Pharisees tried without success to arrest him (John 7:32), they accused him of having a demon (John 8:48) and tried to stone him (John 8:59; 10:31). Finally the high priest gathered together the Sanhedrin, the great religious council of the Jews. He was its president and its other members were all either Pharisees or Sadducees. He advised them to seek the death of Jesus (John 11:47–57), and so from that day onwards, they were looking for a chance to do away with him.

Jesus was well aware of their hatred and their plots. The writer to the Hebrews commented on his patient endurance of such hostility. His readers were beginning to face some persecution in their own stand for Christ. There had been no martyrs in their fellowship yet, though, and so he points them to Christ himself (Hebrews 12:3f.).

Consider him who endured from sinners such hostility against himself, so that you may not grow weary or faint-hearted. In your struggle against sin you have not yet resisted to the point of shedding your blood.

His anticipation of the cross

'Don't worry, it may never happen!' Hardly the gospel, and yet it must be said with shame that posters with hardly more of the good news sometimes appear outside churches. Despite its obvious lack of real hope, this pathetic piece of counsel does contain the only ray of future light in the minds of some people. They are haunted by gloomy thoughts of what may be their lot tomorrow, or next week, or next year, and their comfort lies in the thought that things may not turn out to be so bad after all. They do not hope in God, only in a change of circumstances.

What about Jesus Christ? What was his outlook on the future? Of course, he was trusting in God, for he is the perfect example of faith as well as its perfect object. He knew, however, long before the crucifixion, that he was going to have to suffer and die. Calvary existed in his mind, in his imagination, in all the anticipation of its dreadful agonies, long before he was nailed to the tree. The expectation of suffering is itself suffering.

Some writers of the past have used the phrase 'Galilean springtime' about the early part of Jesus' ministry. They visualized it as a time when great crowds thronged him, when everybody listened to his teaching with bated breath and when the thought of suffering and death was never in his mind. He would conquer the whole nation, and perhaps the whole world, by his teaching. Only later, when the crowds began to leave him, did he anticipate a tragic end to his life.

This picture is just not true to the facts. Certainly the Galilean crowds were often large. Certainly the realization of the cost of discipleship only began to take its toll and to cut down the numbers after a while. But the cross was by no means an afterthought. Early in his ministry Jesus, using something familiar to his hearers, spoke of himself as the bridegroom. He said, 'Can the wedding guests fast while the bridegroom is with them? As long as they have the bridegroom with them, they cannot fast. The days will come, when the bridegroom is taken away from them, and then they will fast in that day.' (Mark 2:19f.) The language here suggests violence. The parable of the sower too anticipates persecution and tribulation for the followers of Jesus (Mark 4:17); if it were to face them, would their Master escape it?

These hints of a destiny of suffering are followed later by absolutely clear and plain teaching. At Caesarea Philippi, Jesus had asked his disciples who they believed him to be. Peter had replied, 'You are the Christ, the son of the living God.' (Matthew 16:16). Straight away Jesus began to teach them what sort of Christ he was to be. 'From that time Jesus began to show his disciples that he must go to Jerusalem and suffer many things from the elders and chief priests and scribes, and be killed, and on the third day be raised.' (Matthew 16:21). This was a definite course of teaching, which seems to have become more and more detailed as time went on. 'Behold, we are going up to Jerusalem; and the Son of man will be delivered to the chief priests and scribes, and they will condemn him to death, and deliver him to the Gentiles to be mocked and scourged and crucified.' (Matthew 20:17ff.) Mark, introducing this same saying, pictures Jesus walking some distance ahead of the disciples, who were huddled behind him in amazement and fear (Mark 10:32ff.). They were walking to Jerusalem; he was anticipating Calvary.

Jesus spoke of his destiny as undergoing a baptism or drinking a cup (Mark 10:38), and these images suggest suffering and sorrow (Psalm 69:1–3; Isaiah 51:17). His ministry had opened with baptism in water; it was to close with baptism in blood. How he felt about this becomes clear when we hear him cry out, 'I have a baptism to be baptized with; and how I am constrained until it is accomplished!' (Luke 12:50.) This was his destiny, and, as the word translated 'constrained' suggests, he felt hemmed in and under constant pressure because of this.

Gethsemane

From time to time the church has been plagued by heresies in which either the deity or the humanity of Jesus has been denied or under-valued. Sometimes it has been suggested that he was not a real man, but only a kind of phantom. No such theory can be entertained for a single moment if we take the events in the garden of Gethsemane seriously. Study them in any of the gospels that record them (Matthew 26:36–56; Mark 14:32–50; Luke 22:39–53).

Mark gives us a particularly vivid account of what happened on that occasion. He tells us that Jesus 'took with him Peter and James and John, and began to be greatly distressed and troubled.' (Mark 14:33.) Commentators are agreed that this sentence is not easy to translate into English. The language is strong, very strong, and no English verb quite expresses either of the two Greek verbs involved. Distress, horror, dread, amazement – all are involved. Out of this horrifying experience came a poignant word to his disciples, 'My soul is very sorrowful, even to death;' (Mark 14:34). These words too are so very difficult to translate. The New English Bible rendering is rather free, but it does more justice to them as an expression of deep feeling: 'My heart is ready to break with grief.'

It was while his heart was thus weighed down with horror and grief that Jesus went to pray. 'Abba, Father, all things are possible to thee; remove this cup from me; yet not what I will, but what thou wilt.' (Mark 14:36.) The use of the word 'cup' in such a context as this makes us realize what an agony of anticipation must have formed the emotional background to its use by him on earlier occasions. His human nature shrank from the cross, yet his will embraced the Father's will. He would do what the Father wanted him to do, no matter what the cost of it might be to him.

In Gethsemane, he was denied the human comfort his disciples might have given at this time. Some of them had said, so glibly, that they could drink the cup he was to drink and undergo a baptism with him (Mark 10:38f.), yet when the time came, he had to face it alone. Not only did they fail to understand what it meant for him. They could not even keep their eyes open!

Calvary

> But none of the ransomed ever knew
> How deep were the waters crossed;
> Nor how dark was the night that the Lord passed through,
> Ere he found His sheep that was lost.

In these words, Ira D. Sankey speaks for us all. There are depths of suffering in the cross of the Lord Jesus Christ that none of us can hope to plumb. One of the most unexpected and impressive features of the gospels is the fact that their authors make no attempt to exploit the emotional impact of the events. What might the sensational press of today have done? What about the cheap modern novel? Even great writers like Shakespeare, Tolstoy or Goethe would have been sorely tempted to dwell on particular aspects of the physical or inner sufferings of the figure on the centre cross. The gospel writers simply record the facts, with economy of language, and allow them to speak for themselves — and how they speak!

We shall simply ponder two great utterances that came from the lips of the Saviour himself as he hung on the Roman cross, because they tell us all we need to know. John records that Jesus said, 'I thirst' (John 19:28). In these words all the physical agonies of the cross were focused, for a raging thirst always overtook a victim of crucifixion after he had spent some hours on his cross.

This we can say, but who can hope to penetrate beyond the surface of the most awful cry ever to emerge from the lips of a human being? 'My God, my God, why hast thou forsaken me?' Luke and John each record three sayings from the cross, but Matthew (27:46) and Mark (15:34) give us this only. It must have impressed them so greatly that they allowed it to stand completely alone — like the lonely experience out of which it came — in their accounts of the crucifixion.

To explore the meaning of this saying with any fullness would be to move beyond the bounds of our subject. Suffering in the place of sinners, taking the punishment that was due to us, knowing in his experience the agonies of the lost, although he was absolutely pure from sin and was the very Son of God – it is along lines such as these our thoughts must move if we are to take these words seriously in the light of his other teaching. For any human being, to be forsaken by God represents the unthinkable, even though it is exactly what our sins deserve, and what they will receive unless we turn to the Saviour. But for the sinner it is in fact the logical outcome of a life of sin, and represents the making permanent of his condition along with all the penalties which must accompany it eternally. For Christ, however, it was the very opposite of what he deserved, and represented an awful break in that fellowship which he had known with his Father, not simply throughout his sinless life, but from all eternity. What suffering! What love!

8

ALIVE FOR EVERMORE!

Life is for living. How good it is to be alive! God has set us in his own universe, in a world full of interest. Everywhere we go we find colour, sound, order, beauty, majestic sights, delicate detail. There is food to eat, water to drink, work to do, air to breathe, and there are people to meet, to love, to serve. It is all there, out there in the world. And what of myself? I have eyes to see it all, ears to hear it all, hands to handle it, feet to walk about it, and a heart to love.

But! But at the end comes death! Life leaves me and I leave this setting – for what? Somebody has well said that any true view of life must begin with a true view of death. Yet the impression we so often get is that people are trying very hard not to think about it. Sex used to be the forbidden topic of conversation, but now it is death. Yet experience has a way of breaking this conspiracy of silence, and we have to face it, if only for a few days.

To spell the matter out more clearly, it is not simply dying that people are afraid of, but death. Dying may fill us with fear but we know that, however unpleasant the mode of it may be, it will soon be over. It is what comes after it that really puts terror in the heart, what the epistle to the Hebrews calls 'a fearful prospect of judgement' (Hebrews 10:27). This is the real sting of death.

Now death in fact casts its shadow over life. The opening paragraph of this chapter may well have seemed to some readers to be quite unrealistic. What about disease, sorrow, suffering in all its forms? What about the thorns and the thistles, the earthquakes, the floods? What about those whose eyes and ears do not function or who can never use their legs to walk about this grand creation? Then there is the great fact which the Bible takes with such seriousness, far more seriously than most human beings – the fact of sin, that is, man's rebellion against his Creator. What about man's inhumanity to man, his cruelty, his greed, his lust for another man's wife or another man's goods? Most of all, what about his failure to give God thanks for all he has made and his determination to do his own will, come hell or high water, and not the will of him to whom he owes everything?

In fact, the word 'death' in the Bible covers not simply the absence of physical life, but all the consequences of man's sin, and especially the condition of enmity against God and his purposes which we all find in ourselves if we probe deeply enough. God prescribed a very simple test for man to see if he really loved him and would do his will. He warned him, 'in the day that you eat of it you shall die' (Genesis 2:17), and die he did in this spiritual sense. He was dead towards God. This death began to work in his whole being and eventually physical death claimed him.

Foretold in Scripture

We often think of Christ's resurrection as a great miracle, and so of course it is. But we do not think enough about the amazing fact that one who was God in the flesh actually entered the experience of death. He was not only divine but also absolutely pure from sin – but he came to carry the penalty of sin for us, and this penalty is death.

In his teaching, he was constantly seeking to get his disciples to take in the fact of his coming death, but they were completely bewildered and did not accept it. Peter said to him, 'God forbid, Lord! This shall never happen to you.' (Matthew 16:22.) This brought a very sharp rebuke from Jesus. Because they did not take in the fact of his death they did not grasp the complementary fact of his resurrection, which he so often linked with that death (e.g. Matthew 16:21; 17:22f.; 20:17–19). In fact, the angels who met the disciples at the empty tomb on Easter morning gently rebuked them (Luke 24:5ff.):

> Why do you seek the living among the dead? Remember how he told you, while he was still in Galilee, that the Son of man must be delivered into the hands of sinful men, and be crucified, and on the third day rise. (Luke 24:5ff.)

The resurrection was not foretold only in Jesus' teaching, of course, but also in the Old Testament. Paul preached in a Jewish synagogue in Thessalonica. Luke tells us (Acts 17:2f.):

> Paul went in, as was his custom, and for three weeks [i.e. sabbaths] he argued with them from the scriptures, explaining and proving that it was necessary for the Christ to suffer and to rise from the dead, and saying, 'This Jesus, whom I proclaim to you, is the Christ.'

It has been suggested that on the first sabbath he may have explained from the Old Testament that the Messiah must suffer, that on the second he showed from the same source that he must rise from the dead, and that on the third he moved from prophecy to recent history and proclaimed to them that these things had now been fulfilled in Jesus the Christ.

What Old Testament passages would the early Christians use to show this? We do not know in any extensive way, but we do know that they recognized Isaiah 52:13 – 53:12 to be fulfilled in Christ. This passage certainly implies that God's suffering servant was going to be raised from the dead. It speaks clearly of death (Isaiah 53:8f., 12), and yet it also states, 'Behold my servant shall prosper, he shall be exalted and lifted up, and shall be very high. . . . I will divide him a portion with the great, and he shall divide the spoil with the strong; because he poured out his soul to death.' (Isaiah 52:13; 53:12.) Read this great passage and then read on through chapters 54 and 55. They have a wonderful atmosphere of joy, so appropriate as they follow a declaration of full atonement and glorious resurrection.

Likewise Peter took Psalm 16, argued that it must apply not to David who wrote it but rather to Christ, and then showed that it foretold his resurrection from the dead (Acts 2:24–32).

Miraculous in nature

Let us be quite clear about it. We are talking about the *resurrection* of Jesus. We are not talking about his 'survival' of death in some vague way. We are not talking about appearances of his 'ghost'. We are certainly not talking simply about his continued influence in the world. We are talking about the resurrection of his dead body, about his personal victory over death, about a tomb that was empty, not because the body had dissolved but because he was gloriously alive again. We are using the term 'resurrection' in its normal dictionary meaning, 'restoration to life'.

Now this is plainly a miracle. It is true that there are a few examples of the dead being raised both in the Old Testament and in the New (1 Kings 17:17–24; 2 Kings 4:32–37; Mark 5:35–43; Luke 7:11–17; John 11:1–44; Acts 20:7–12). These too are miracles, but they are not of the same order as his resurrection, as we shall see. Nevertheless if there is one thing we all recognize it is that in all normal circumstances death is the end of life as we know it.

The Lord Jesus performed many miracles himself. The gospels record in detail quite a number of them. Many of them deal with diseases of various kinds, or with cases of demon possession. In such phenomena death casts its shadow before it, and Christ's touch of life banished some part of that shadow. But in his resurrection, Christ was both the subject and the object of the greatest miracle, and he dealt with no symptom of man's subjection to death, but with death itself.

The apostle Paul gives a most interesting and helpful list of the resurrection appearances of the Saviour. This is found in 1 Corinthians 15:5–8, and it is a very impressive list. It gives two appearances to the twelve apostles. These were the men who had been so devastated by the death of their master and who had never taken in the promise of his resurrection. They include James, a member of his own family who rejected his claims during his ministry (John 7:5). There was an appearance to a great crowd of five hundred. Surely in such a crowd there would be some hard-headed realists who would be satisfied with

nothing short of real, tangible evidence? Then Paul too saw
him, and his encounter took place during the course of his bitter
campaign against the Christians.

One rather odd piece of evidence is often overlooked or
wrongly estimated. This is the fact that the accounts of the first
Easter day given in the four gospels are not easy to harmonize.
Many have worked at this and proposed different solutions to
the problems, some more helpful than others. But the very
difficulties testify to the fact that we are dealing with indepen-
dent witnesses. The resurrection was vital and central to the
claims Christians made for their Lord. If those claims were
based on a lie, we can be certain that the witnesses would have
taken as much trouble as possible to make certain that their
accounts could be harmonized with ease.

A number of sceptics have set out to study the evidence, with
the clear expectation that it would not stand up to scrutiny,
only to find themselves utterly convinced by the evidence that
Jesus Christ really did emerge from the grave, alive from the
dead. Frank Morison's account of his search *Who Moved the
Stone?* makes compelling reading.

Unique in character

Even as a miracle the resurrection of Jesus stands alone, as he
himself stands alone amongst men. On one occasion, Paul
declared that the subject of his preaching was 'that the Christ
must suffer, and that, by being the first to rise from the dead,
he would proclaim light both to the people and to the Gentiles.'
(Acts 26:23.) Are you puzzled about that word 'first'? What
about those who were restored to life by God through Elijah
(1 Kings 17:17–24) and Elisha (2 Kings 4:32–37)? What about
those whom Jesus himself raised from death during his earthly
ministry (Mark 5:35–43; Luke 7:11–17; John 11:1–44)?

The resurrection of Christ is in fact a miracle of a completely
new order altogether. All those who were raised from the dead
before he died were simply restored to life. People like the
Shunammite's son and the daughter of Jairus resumed life at

the point interrupted temporarily by their death. We would hope their lives bore the marks of what had happened in a deep concern now to show their gratitude to God in the kind of lives they lived. Apart from this, however, it was simply a case of an extended lifespan.

Not so with the Lord Jesus Christ. His resurrection was his emergence into a new sphere of life altogether. His conquest of death was absolute. He was taken out of the very conditions in which death operates. John saw him on the island of Patmos. He was glorious in appearance, and John fell at his feet as though dead (Revelation 1:17f.):

> But he laid his right hand upon me, saying, 'Fear not, I am the first and the last, and the living one; I died, and behold I am alive for evermore, and I have the keys of Death and Hades.

Was his resurrection body physical at all? Yes, it was. He said to the wondering disciples, 'See my hands and my feet, that it is I myself; handle me, and see; for a spirit has not flesh and bones as you see that I have.' (Luke 24:39.) When they still wondered, he took some food and ate it in their presence. Thomas, an absentee when the Saviour first appeared to the disciples as a group, could not accept their story. Eight days later, the Lord Jesus appeared again, when Thomas was present, and said to him, 'Put your finger here, and see my hands; and put out your hand, and place it in my side; do not be faithless, but believing.' (John 20:27.)

God does not play tricks on us. He deals with us according to truth. These passages mean nothing unless we are being taught in them that the body of Jesus after the resurrection was a real one. This is not, however, the whole story. The conditions of his life were changed. He did not need to knock at the door of the upper room to gain admittance. He simply appeared. He made himself known in two different ways. We get the impression that during the forty days between his resurrection and ascension he looked much as he had always done. The two on the road to Emmaus did not recognize him at first, because God prevented them from doing so (Luke 24:16), but they treated him as if he were simply an ordinary human being. Paul and John saw him revealed in glorious light and splendour (Acts 9; Revelation 1). Paul speaks of 'his glorious body' (Philippians 3:21), as if this is now its normal state (cf. 1 Corinthians 15:42–44). It is clear, however, that he could if he wished make himself known without the glorious aura of light in which Paul and John saw him.

Divine in power

The resurrection could only have been an act of God. Death is man's most dreadful and dreaded enemy. It rules like a king over every human being. Only a stupendous release of divine power could overthrow that enemy. It is perhaps surprising at first to find that when the New Testament writers want to illustrate the power of God, they do not usually talk about the creation of the universe. To bring into being all the varied features of this vast universe and to sustain it all in its ordered course – what power is this! These men do not dwell so much on that as on the resurrection of Christ, which they must have seen as the supreme act of power. Paul prays that his readers may be given divine enlightenment, so that they may know 'what is the immeasurable greatness of his power in us who believe, according to the working of his great might which he accomplished in Christ when he raised him from the dead ...' (Ephesians 1:19f.)

Whose power was it that raised Christ? According to many passages it was the power of God himself, or the power of God the Father. Peter, preaching at Pentecost, declared to his guilty hearers (Acts 2:23f.):

'This Jesus ... you crucified and killed by the hands of lawless men. But God raised him up, having loosed the pangs of death, because it was not possible for him to be held by it.'

Paul says that Christ was raised from the dead by the glory of the Father (Roman 6:4; cf, Galatians 1:1; 1 Peter 1:3).

That would seem then to settle the question, but does it?

Not really. In John 2:19–21, the evangelist records a saying of Jesus and the reaction of the Jews to it, and then adds a comment of his own:

> Jesus answered them, 'Destroy this temple, and in three days I will raise it up.' The Jews then said, 'It has taken forty-six years to build this temple, and will you raise it up in three days?' But he spoke of the temple of his body.

Later, he said of his life, 'I have power to lay it down, and I have power to take it again.' (John 10:18.) So Christ emerged from the grave by virtue of his own power!

Even this does not settle the issue. In Romans 8:11, Paul's words probably imply that the Spirit of God had his function too in the resurrection.

> If the Spirit of him who raised Jesus from the dead dwells in you, he who raised Christ Jesus from the dead will give life to your mortal bodies also through his Spirit which dwells in you.

The New Testament therefore seems to speak not with one voice but with three on this most important question. This is however just what we ought to have expected. If the Bible really contains the doctrine of the Trinity, then it means that the Father, the Son and the Holy Spirit are one in their nature, and therefore are completely united in their purpose. They do not act against each other. Rather, they work together in all they do. So this most important act of God was brought about by the power of the triune God.

Far-reaching in results

It is important to notice not only what the Bible teaches but also what it emphasizes. It is very easy to go wrong if we do not study this. Many false sects have started with something that belongs to the circumference of the Christian faith, have put it in the centre, displacing Christ himself, and so have distorted and undermined the whole gospel.

Now the New Testament writers lay very great emphasis

indeed upon the death and resurrection of Christ. Paul says
(1 Corinthians 15:3f.):

> I delivered to you as of first importance what I also received, that
> Christ died for our sins in accordance with the scriptures, that he
> was buried, that he was raised on the third day in accordance with
> the scriptures.

The space given to these events in the four gospels speaks for
itself. Matthew, Mark and Luke each give about one third of
their space to the events of passion week, and John goes further
still, with nearly half of all his material devoted to it.

Why so much emphasis on the resurrection? The victory of
Christ over death showed that God had accepted his sacrifice
for our sins. Paul says that Jesus 'was put to death for our
trespasses and raised for our justification' (Romans 4:25).
Justification really stands for a new relationship with God in
which he treats us, sinners as we are, as if we were in fact
righteous. This does not in fact mean that God turns a blind
eye to the truth. What it means is that because Christ has carried
our punishment, we can go free from it, and we can stand before
God as if we were faultless. We might have expected Paul here
to connect justification with Christ's death. He links it with
his resurrection, because it is only through this that we are given
the assurance that the sacrifice was accepted by God. As he
puts it elsewhere, in a chapter worth reading right through
because of its teaching about resurrection, 'If Christ has not
been raised, your faith is futile and you are still in your sins.'
(1 Corinthians 15:17.)

The resurrection of Christ throws a marvellous light across
the whole of his life and all the claims he made. The gospels
contain so many of his claims. Is he really the Son of God,
the Son of Man, the long expected Messiah, the great Servant
of the Lord, the Saviour and Judge of men? If he is still in
the grave, not one of these claims could have been true. But
he was brought out of the tomb by the great power of God,
and so God himself signified in this way that all his claims were
genuine. He was 'designated Son of God in power according

to the Spirit of holiness by his resurrection from the dead' (Romans 1:4).

What a lot of promises Jesus made during the course of his ministry! He told his disciples that he would be with them (Matthew 18:20), that he would send the Holy Spirit to them (John 16:7) and that he would come back again (John 14:3). These promises and many others like them could never be fulfilled without the resurrection of him who made them. The Epistle to the Hebrews contains only one express reference to the resurrection of Christ (13:20), but its great doctrine of the heavenly priesthood of Jesus and his constant intercession for his people makes no sense at all unless he rose from the dead and is in heaven now.

Because Christ has overcome death, so shall we. To be 'in Christ', that is in living union with him as a Christian believer, is to be deeply involved in all that he did. Paul, in Romans 6 and elsewhere, teaches that when the Lord Jesus Christ died on the cross and rose from the dead, this meant the death and resurrection of each one who is joined to him. This has two stages to it. First of all, we 'die' to what displeases God and we 'rise again' to a new life in which we do what we know he wants us to do. Then, if Christ returns after we have died, we are raised up with a glorious body like his (Philippians 3:21). All this happens only because he has first died and risen again, and so it is really the fruit of his work.

It is no wonder that the men of the New Testament got so excited about his victory over death!

9

FAR ABOVE ALL

Young people today often have a real 'hang-up' on the question of authority. They tend to resent parents, policemen, teachers, employers and royalty. Why is this? Is it because they do not accept the idea of authority at all? Not really. If it were this, then there would never be a gang with a leader. The real problem is often not the authority itself but the way it is exercised, or the way they think it will be exercised. So in this case, it is not so much authority as 'authoritarianism' that is the real issue.

This certainly over-simplifies things, but is there not something in it? What folk are so often looking for is a leader they can really trust, somebody who is fit to lead, not just because he is strong (although that is certainly needed) but because he has the real interests of the group at heart. They may not know who it is for whom they are seeking, but the New Testament writers do. They tell us his name is Jesus. He is supreme, he loves us, and he works for our good from the place of absolute power.

Taken up into heaven

Luke is a very important writer. He is important because he is the only non-Jew to have his writings included in the New Testament. He is important because he wrote more of it than anybody else, for even Paul, with all his letters, does not contribute as much on a page for page basis. He is important too because he gives us the facts about the ascension of the Lord Jesus, and does so in both his books.

He tells the story very simply in the last chapter of his gospel (24:50f.):

> Then he led them out as far as Bethany, and lifting up his hands he blessed them. While he blessed them, he parted from them.

This very brief account is supplemented in the Acts of the Apostles. 'As they were looking on, he was lifted up, and a cloud took him out of their sight.' (Acts 1:9.) The received ending of the gospel of Mark makes reference to this also. 'So then the Lord Jesus, after he had spoken to them, was taken up into heaven, and sat down at the right hand of God.' (Mark 16:19.)

Now it is sometimes said that the ascension rests upon far too little evidence. The authenticity of the latter half of Mark chapter 16 has been disputed, and so it is maintained that only Luke tells the story, and that we cannot accept it simply upon the evidence of one man. To say this, however, is completely to misread the facts. It may be that, apart from the disputed reference in Mark 16, only Luke records the historical facts, but then this is true of almost everything in the Acts of the Apostles. Yet men as diverse as Sir William Ramsay and Adolph Harnack have tested Luke's reliability as an historian and have not found him wanting.

But there is much more to be said. Peter speaks of 'the resurrection of Jesus Christ, who has gone into heaven and is at the right hand of God (1 Peter 3:21f.). It is worth noting, incidentally, the way Peter puts it. He does not say that he was taken up into heaven (however true that might have been) but that he has 'gone' into heaven, as though this was his own act. If the resurrection could be viewed as the work both of the Father and of the Son, so could the ascension. Theologians may make a distinction between the ascension and the heavenly session, that is, between the actual entry of Christ into heaven and the fact that he is still there reigning in the place of power. Although this distinction is valid, the two really belong together. It was because he ascended that he is now able to reign from heaven. Paul surely presupposes the ascension when he speaks of the power of God that 'raised him from the dead and made him sit at his right hand in the heavenly places' (Ephesians 1:20). The writer to the Hebrews, too, tells us that 'Christ has entered ... into heaven itself' (Hebrews 9:24). This is a fully authenticated piece of Bible history, not by any means resting upon the testimony of only one writer.

Seated in the place of power

There have been many absolute monarchs, some of them tyrants without any real concern for the welfare of their subjects. Mercifully, they have reigned only over a restricted area and only for a certain length of time. Louis XIV of France may have reigned longer than any other European king, but the time to die came for him too.

How different with Christ! His kingdom is both universal (without limits of territory) and eternal (without limits of time). This is really what the terms of the Old Testament vision were (Daniel 7:13f.):

> I saw in the night visions, and behold, with the clouds of heaven there came one like a son of man, and he came to the Ancient of Days and was presented before him. And to him was given dominion and glory and kingdom, that all peoples, nations, and languages should serve him; his dominion is an everlasting dominion, which shall not pass away, and his kingdom one that shall not be destroyed.

The Lord Jesus never had any doubt that this was to be his destiny. Although he spoke frequently about his cross, the subject of the kingdom was very often on his lips. At what must have seemed to his close followers the moment when the plans for the kingdom went into total eclipse, he declared to the high priest, 'But I tell you, hereafter you will see the Son of man seated at the right hand of Power, and coming on the clouds of heaven.' (Matthew 26:64.) The reference to Daniel's prophecy is unmistakable.

We must not make the mistake of thinking that his kingdom belongs to the future and only to the future. It is quite true it has not yet entered its final stage, but it is nevertheless a present reality. One day everybody will be aware of that kingdom. Today it can be seen only by the eye of faith. When he was on earth, the Pharisees asked him when the kingdom of God was coming. His answer was 'the kingdom of God is in the midst of you' (Luke 17:21). Wherever the king is, there is the kingdom. God's great king was standing before them but they did not know him. If the kingdom existed even then, it must still exist. The writer to the Hebrews often tells us that Christ sat down when his work was finished: 'When he had made purification for sins, he sat down at the right hand of the Majesty on high.' (Hebrews 1:3.) Later in the same chapter (verse 8) he applies the words of a psalm to him, 'Thy throne, O God, is for ever and ever, the righteous sceptre is the sceptre of thy kingdom.'

This is tremendously encouraging to the Christian. This world is not in the hands of any bully who can seize great power for a while and lord it over his unwilling subjects. It is in the hands of Christ. So the Christian who has to live under tyranny can commit his cause to him in the sure knowledge that he is almighty.

The head of his church

The Bible is full of illustrations. These are far more frequent even than appears to the English reader, because there are a good many hidden away in the original Greek and Hebrew. For example, Old Testament verbs for faith have different meanings. Faith is 'resting on', or 'leaning on', or 'taking refuge in', and so on. Each of these expressions calls a picture to mind. Now this is certainly true of the church in the New Testament. It is the family the Lord loves, the field he cultivates, the temple he is building, the bride he marries. There are many, many more, each presenting some aspect of the church's life and its relationship to Christ. We need to take all of them together to get a complete picture.

Perhaps the most important of them all, certainly in Paul's teaching, is the body. When he was confronted by the risen

Christ on the Damascus road, the glorious one said to him, 'Saul, Saul, why do you persecute me?' (Acts 9:4.) Paul must have been deeply impressed by these words, which contain an identification of the Lord Jesus with his persecuted church. It is not surprising then that he writes so much about the organic union of Christ with his church in terms of a head and a body.

Because he is the head, supreme lordship in the church must always be his. In fact, as Luke tells us in Acts, it is the sovereign Lord who adds members to the church through his work of grace in their hearts (Acts 2:47).

This headship of Christ applies to the whole church and to every aspect of its life (Ephesians 1:20–23):

> [God] raised him from the dead and made him sit at his right hand in the heavenly places, far above all rule and authority and power and dominion, and above every name that is named, not only in this age but also in that which is to come; and he has put all things under his feet and has made him the head over all things for the church, which is his body, the fullness of him who fills all in all.

This means that Christ is ruling the universe with a constant eye on his purpose for his church. All that happens is put to the service of that purpose. What an encouragement for Christians facing persecution, for missionaries who are expelled from the country whose people they love and for us all in the more distressing circumstances of life!

If Christ is the head of the whole church, he is head also of each local church. The book of Revelation, with its vivid picture language, speaks of one like a son of man walking in the midst of the seven golden lampstands (Revelation 1:12f.). It is he therefore that joins them to each other because they are all joined to him. He also holds the seven stars in his right hand (Revelation 1:20), symbolizing his complete power over each of the churches. Because he has this power, he addresses a letter to each of the seven churches separately, related to the particular needs of each of them. He does not hesitate to issue commands they must obey and warnings they must heed as well as promises in which they can rejoice.

If he is indeed the head of the church, then every local

congregation needs to acknowledge what Christians of an earlier generation used to call 'the crown rights of the redeemer', and submit to him in everything. No church can 'go it alone' or 'do its own thing', because each church exists for him and for him alone. It is his purposes that must determine everything that is done in the church. If we really took this seriously, a lot of our church programmes would be given an entirely new look.

Active upon earth

If Christ was taken up into heaven and disappeared from view, does this mean his activity on earth has come to an end – at least until his second coming? By no means! It was just before he left the world that he said, 'Lo, I am with you always, to the close of the age.' (Matthew 28:20.) The age has not yet ended and so the promise holds good today. But if he is in heaven, how can he be still on earth?

This is a good question, and the Bible gives it a wonderful answer. He is still on earth through the Holy Spirit. We may sometimes envy the first disciples their first-hand contact with Jesus of Nazareth. Do not envy them. If you are a Christian, you have a much more intimate relationship with him than they had until the day of Pentecost. The Lord Jesus said to them, just before his death, 'I will not leave you desolate; I will come to you.' (John 14:18.) In the verses immediately before this statement he had been speaking to them about the Holy Spirit. He promised to give him to them so that he might be with them for ever.

This promise was fulfilled on the day of Pentecost. Referring to the events of that day, Peter declared, 'Being therefore exalted at the right hand of God, and having received from the Father the promise of the Holy Spirit, he has poured out this which you see and hear.' (Acts 2:33.) This means that there is a special connection between the exaltation of the Lord Jesus and the gift of the Holy Spirit. He was exalted because his work of dealing with our sins had been completed. The Holy Spirit is sent from heaven to make this salvation from sin wonderfully real in the hearts of all his people.

This is not the place for us to study the work of the Holy Spirit in detail. Another volume in this series explores that great theme. It is important, however, for us to realize that although the exalted Christ and the Holy Spirit can be distinguished from each other they cannot be separated. The three persons of the Trinity always work together. You and I, as Christians, are 'in Christ' – see how often Paul uses that phrase and its equivalents in Ephesians 1:1–14 – and so are in living union with him. It is also true that the Holy Spirit dwells in us, but one of his names is 'the Spirit of Christ' (Romans 8:9), so that Christ is really living in us through the Spirit. In this way he can be in heaven and on earth at the same time. The idea is a mysterious one, and it does not have any real parallel in human experience, but we would expect the things of God to contain some mysteries, because God is far greater than we are.

So we are not left on our own to live the Christian life. Christ gives us his power through the Spirit. This means that if we depend on him and not on our own ability he will keep us pure, will enable us to do his will, and will use us in his service. In this way, the living Christ is still active on earth. To surrender everything to Christ and submit to his absolute kingship is to enable him to fill us with his Spirit, so that our lives will bring him the glory that is his right, and which we wish him to have because he has done so much for us.

Praying for his people

Every Christian man lives two lives. There is his life amongst men, in his family, at his work, moving amongst his friends and acquaintances. There is also his life with God, the relationship of worship and love and prayer which operates inside him. The quality of the former is always determined by the quality of the latter.

In the Lord Jesus each of these two lives was perfect, and

the two were perfectly integrated. The gospel writers, and especially Luke, give us much insight into his prayer-life. We see him praying at the great crisis points in his ministry (e.g. Luke 3:21; 9:28f.; 22:40–46). It was not only in such times of special need, however, that he prayed, but throughout his day-to-day life. It was their observance of his own life of prayer that caused the disciples to ask him to give them instruction in prayer (Luke 11:1).

One of the most selfless expressions of prayer is intercession. In it we take the needs of other people on our hearts and bring them to God. Simon, along with the other disciples, was to face a great crisis in his own life when the Saviour was taken from him to death. He said to his disciple (Luke 22:31f.):

> Simon, Simon, behold, Satan demanded to have you, that he might sift you like wheat, but I have prayed for you that your faith may not fail; and when you have turned again, strengthen your brethren.

The most wonderful of all his prayers is to be found in John 17. There we find him interceding for his disciples in the simplest and yet deepest terms. What an encouragement it is to find that we are included in the prayer, for he said, 'I do not pray for these only, but also for those who believe in me through their word,' (John 17:20). Their word has come down to us in written form in the New Testament, and so this prayer includes us.

What has all this to do with the exaltation of Christ? A very great deal. The letter to the Hebrews has a lot to say about the priestly function of the Lord Jesus. Now a study of the Old Testament reveals to us that the main job of a priest was to offer sacrifice. The writer of this great letter never tires of telling us that Christ has done that for us, and done it with complete effectiveness and finality. He sat down, not only because he is a king, but also because his sacrificial work has been completed (Hebrews 10:11–14). But a priest was called to pray as well as to offer sacrifice. Christ is still our high priest and he is occupied constantly in prayer. As the writer puts it, so triumphantly, 'He is able for all time to save those who draw

near to God through him, since he always lives to make intercession for them.' (Hebrews 7:25.)

This theme is not restricted to the letter to the Hebrews.
John, in his first letter, says, 'My little children, I am writing
this to you so that you may not sin; but if any one does sin,
we have an advocate with the Father, Jesus Christ the righteous;'
(1 John 2:1). Paul, in a deeply emotional passage, asks the
question, 'Who is to condemn? Is it Christ Jesus, who died,
yes, who was raised from the dead, who is at the right hand
of God, who indeed intercedes for us?' (Romans 8:34.) We get
the feeling that each successive fact is more wonderful to him
than its predecessor, and that his thought reaches its highest
point with his assertion that Christ is praying for us.

How much do we really think about this? When the devil
seems to be throwing everything against you, when you are over-
whelmed by some sorrow, when you pass through some
experience of deep discouragement, remember this. He is
praying! Others may promise to pray and forget, but not the
Saviour. He is praying for you – now!

Coming back again

The Christian life is a life of faith. We know Christ, love him
and serve him, but we have never seen him. Yet to us, he is
not simply a figure in history, but somebody who lives now
and who has brought us into a wonderful relationship with him,
which is vibrant with life and power. Yet we long to see him.
Shall we be denied this for ever? No, the Word of God promises
that he will come again.

What will he do when he returns? He will take us to be with
him (John 14:1–3; Philippians 1:23; 1 Thessalonians 4:16f.).
Most Christians will of course be dead, but many will be alive
at the time of his return. Some will be taken from death and
some from life, but both groups will be given bodies like his
own glorious body (Philippians 3:21). As Paul puts it in one
passage, 'When Christ who is our life appears, then you also
will appear with him in glory.' (Colossians 3:4.) We can hardly

conceive what this will mean. Paul wrote a long chapter on the subject of the resurrection of believers (1 Corinthians 15) and this, as we have noted, repays careful study. The implications of it all are simply staggering. To think that we shall still have bodies and yet that these will be freed from the limitations of earth and will be perfectly adapted to the new dimensions of life God has for us in eternity! How we shall praise him then!

What else will happen? The whole of human history has known injustice, evil men apparently getting away with acts of great cruelty, cursing God and refusing to do his will. Sometimes God has judged them within the process of history, but sometimes it seems as though he has not. They seem to go on their way into blacker and blacker crimes, heedless of him and of his claims on all human life. Can this go on for ever? No! The Bible tells us a lot about historical judgements but it also tells us about a great future judgement which everyone will have to face.

The Lord Jesus told his disciples that he would judge the world when he returned. 'The Son of man is to come with his angels in the glory of his Father, and then he will repay every man for what he has done.' (Matthew 16:27.) The New Testament writers take up this teaching and amplify it. Paul speaks of the time 'when the Lord Jesus is revealed from heaven with his mighty angels in flaming fire, inflicting vengeance upon those who do not know God and upon those who do not obey the gospel of our Lord Jesus' (2 Thessalonians 1:7f.). This gives great seriousness to the proclamation of the good news of the Lord Jesus Christ, and every Christian ought to regard this as a priority of the highest kind for his own life.

The true Christian longs for the Lord Jesus to come back. John, in the book of Revelation, using one of the illustrations of the church, declares, 'The Spirit and the Bride say, "Come."' A few verses later he writes, 'He who testifies to these things says, "Surely I am coming soon." Amen. Come, Lord Jesus!' (Revelation 22:17, 20.) When he came to earth the first time the human beings he had made mocked and rejected him, and killed him. He is coming to be vindicated by his Father in the very scene where he had been rejected. Nothing could be more fitting. 'Come, Lord Jesus!'

10

THE MYSTERY OF HIS PERSON

The person who has had all his questions answered and who can now see that the universe has no mysteries does not exist. Everybody, just everybody, is perplexed about something. In fact, we seem to need some mysteries to satisfy one side of our make-up. Years ago, I met an old man out in the country. We were talking about the beauties of nature, and I said, in reply to some comment of his, 'That's wonderful!' 'Wonderful, young man?' said he; 'Everything's wonderful!'

That old man had not lost the wonderment and enquiring mind of a child. In a child everything raises questions. Why this? Why that? How does this work? What does this mean? As we get older, our questions may become less clamorous but we are still just as puzzled. We may be able to understand gravity or electricity, but what about DNA? What about the relationship between the mind and the body? What about the presence of evil in the world?

Many of the deepest questions we ask are about the meaning of life itself. The philosopher Schopenhauer was seated one day on a park bench. Seeing this elderly, shabbily dressed man and thinking him a tramp, a policeman accosted him. 'What are you doing here?' he asked. 'I wish I knew,' replied the philosopher, 'for I have given the best years of my life to that problem and do not know the answer yet.'

There is one mystery that many have found provides the clue to many of life's other problems. It is well expressed in the words of the disciples of Jesus Christ, when, after they had

witnessed a miracle, they asked, 'Who then is this, that even
the wind and sea obey him?' Those who encountered him could
not help asking questions, and they found the answers to be
so wonderful that from then on everything in life and everything in the universe looked different.

A real man

Martin Luther used to maintain that the proper way to come
to a proper understanding of Jesus Christ was to begin with
his humanity. This was in fact the way the earliest apostles came.
Although their eventual view of his person was the same in
substance as that of Paul, the way they came to it was different.
For them, the supremely wonderful thing was that the Jesus
of Nazareth whom they had known and loved for three years
was exalted in heaven and was the very Lord of all. To Paul,
the supreme wonder lay in the fact that the heavenly Lord who
met him on the Damascus Road had in fact lived a human life
on earth. It is a difference of perspective.

What then do we learn about Jesus the man? We learn that
his manhood was real. He bore all the marks of real and genuine
humanity. Luke tells the story of his birth and gives a glimpse
into his boyhood. After this he tells us, 'And Jesus increased
in wisdom and in stature, and in favour with God and man.'
(Luke 2:52.) He ate and drank, was weary and showed emotions
like joy and sadness, anger and compassion. We saw in chapter
7 how deeply he experienced sorrow and suffering. If he was
not a real man, then the gospels are totally unreliable as historical
documents.

But there are other elements of humanity in his life which
are not always given the recognition they deserve. This
particularly applies to his prayer-life. It is only human beings
who pray. It is quite true that there were very deep dimensions
to his praying, and that he appears to have known God in a
particularly deep way. But these are special qualities in an
experience which was genuinely human. It is only a dependent
being who prays, for it is only a dependent being who needs

help from God. The prayer-life of the Saviour shows every evidence of being as real as other elements in his life. In fact, in Gethsemane prayer and suffering were merged into one. 'Being in an agony he prayed more earnestly; and his sweat became like great drops of blood falling down upon the ground.' (Luke 22:44.)

The gospel of John records a great deal of his teaching. One phrase occurs over and over again in its pages, and is highly relevant to our subject. He described God as 'him who sent me' (John 4:34; 5:23f., *et al.*). In fact, after 'Father' and 'God' this is the most frequent designation of the Almighty to be found in this gospel. He lived his life therefore as the agent of somebody else, determined to do his will and to walk in his ways. This too shows real manhood.

We also find him asking questions. It is quite true that many of them were rhetorical and did not expect an answer. Others were intended to make his hearers think deeply about him and his teaching. Others however seem to have been asked with a genuine desire to know. When confronted with a demoniac boy, he asked the father, 'How long has he had this?' (Mark 9:21.) When Lazarus was in his grave, he asked, 'Where have you laid him?' (John 11:34.) These would seem to be perfectly straightforward questions asked with no motive other than a desire for information.

One striking saying takes us further still. Mark 13 contains much of his teaching about the future, and especially about his second coming. Towards the close of it, he says to his disciples, 'But of that day or that hour no one knows, not even the angels in heaven, nor the Son, but only the Father.' (Mark 13:32.) For the moment we shall simply note this, but shall consider it much more fully in the next chapter.

Here then is a man. A most wonderful person, yes, but despite that, a real man, with flesh and blood, hands and feet, thoughts and feelings, coming to maturity of growth by increase in size and accumulation of knowledge, and then taking the Jerusalem road that led to arrest, mockery, scourging, brutal execution and death. And it was a real man they took down from the tree and put in the grave – and a real man that came out of it!

Far more than man

We cannot stop at this point. The evidence compels us to go further, much further. It is difficult to read through a single passage in any of the gospels without coming to the conclusion that Jesus Christ was more than man.

Think, for example, about his miracles. Now it is quite true he is not the only worker of miracles in the Bible. There were miracles performed by God through Moses and Joshua, through Elijah and Elisha and other characters of Old Testament Scripture. Some of them even restored people to life. It is not any single miracle he performed, but the sum-total of them that points beyond mere humanity. The frequency and the fullness of range of this man's miracles are simply staggering. The impression is given that he was able to exercise control over any and every situation he found. Even when Mark tells us that 'he could do no mighty work there', it is clear from the context that it was their unbelief that stopped him, so that it was morally, not physically, impossible for him to do it. God had joined blessing and faith and he would not divorce them.

This combination of miracles is utterly without parallel in the Old Testament. But the supreme miracle, as we have already seen (chapter 8), was one he performed not on nature nor on other human beings but upon himself. He rose from the dead. By our own power most of us cannot lift ourselves off the ground for more than a few seconds, let alone out of the grave and from the grip of death.

Then there was his teaching. Officers sent by the religious leaders of Israel were instructed to arrest him. On their empty-handed return, the chief priests and Pharisees said to them, 'Why did you not bring him?' They answered, 'No man ever spoke like this man!' (John 7:45f.) It is true that the Holy Spirit had been inspiring human beings and giving them truth to teach and words in which to teach it for many centuries. The Old

Testament is the product of this work of inspiration. But the teaching of Christ possessed some unique features. Once again, as with his miracles, it is the fullness and comprehensiveness of it that strikes us.

More than this, however, is the manner in which he conveyed this teaching to men. Uninspired rabbis were for ever quoting other rabbis, inspired writers often gave the source of their inspiration, by the use of phrases like 'the word of the Lord came to me'. But he does not use this kind of language, hallowed though it was. He said, 'Truly I say to you.' Very often, the 'I' in this phrase is emphatic in the original Greek. No earlier teacher had dared to speak in this way, even under the inspiration of the Holy Spirit.

Most significant of all was his perfect character. We thought about this in chapter 6. He was absolutely flawless in his manner of life before men, and enjoyed the most perfect, unbroken fellowship with his Father until that awful experience on the cross when, because he was taking the place of sinners, he endured the wrath of God for us (Matthew 27:46). It has been well said that no miracle he ever did can equal the miracle that he was. He never failed in his duty either to God or man, and loved his Father and human beings with a love that never varied or wavered. As we have seen already, the New Testament writers do not hesitate to use the strongest language about his character. They regarded his holiness of life as absolute.

In Old Testament days, men and women were called to do many different kinds of work in the service of God. There were prophets, priests and kings, there were judges and great national leaders, like Moses and Joshua. What differentiates the Lord Jesus from all who came before him is the fact that in him all the most significant offices are found in one person. He is the supreme servant of God because not only do all these forms of service find their point of focus in him but be performs each with utter perfection. This puts him entirely in a class of his own. This is really what being the *Christ* or *Messiah* means. He is the one who brings the purposes of God for his people to their fulfilment, not only as a great king but as God's great 'man of many parts'. It is sometimes said of an exceptional man that it would take two or three others to replace him. The total resources of the human race could not replace Christ. This makes him unique.

Lord of all

To say that Jesus Christ is man and more than man is true but it is not enough. We must go further and name him as Lord of all. We saw in chapter 2 that the New Testament preachers and writers gave him this title, and in chapter 1 that it also occurs in some of the gospels.

Without doubt, the word *Lord* is used more frequently than any other in the New Testament to indicate the belief of the first Christians that Jesus Christ is divine. The fact that it was used by the Greek translators of the Old Testament to translate the great name of the Almighty made it quite special when used by a Jew. Peter and others were really claiming deity for Jesus Christ in using it. This means we must not only say he was far more than man; we cannot refrain from saying also that he was not less than God.

This use of the term was probably based on the way our Lord himself employed it on one particular occasion. The day of questions (Mark 11:27 – 12:44) took place during the week which came to its climax in the crucifixion. On this day, Jesus was teaching in the Temple of Jerusalem. People came to him with questions. They belonged to different religious and political groups, and many of these questions were clearly intended as traps. He countered every one and answered them with great wisdom. The most important question of the day, however, came at its close, because this was the one he himself put to his hearers (Mark 12:35–37):

> And as Jesus taught in the temple, he said, 'How can the scribes say that the Christ is the son of David? David himself, inspired by the Holy Spirit, declared, "The Lord said to my Lord, Sit at my right hand, till I put thy enemies under thy feet." David himself calls him Lord; so how is he his son?'

Here, in a psalm acknowledged by his hearers to be messianic, the inspired writer calls the Messiah Lord.

Because he is Lord, this means everything in the universe is under his sway. It may be that sinful men do not acknowledge him now, but one day they will have to bow the knee to him and confess him Lord (Philippians 2:9–11). The Christian needs to take Jesus' lordship very seriously in practical terms. In what has been described as the most illogical sentence in the Bible, Peter once said to him, 'No, Lord.' (Acts 10:14.) You just cannot put those two words together without talking nonsense. The Saviour himself put this very pointedly when he said, 'Why do you call me, "Lord, Lord," and not do what I tell you?' (Luke 6:46.)

The lordship of Christ extends far beyond the scope of human life. In his letters, the apostle Paul uses a number of terms denoting authority which appear to have been applied to various angelic beings in his day. In Colossians, he employs them when he says of Christ (Colossians 1:16):

> In him all things were created, in heaven and on earth, visible and invisible, whether thrones or dominions or principalities or authorities – all things were created through him and for him.

Later in the same letter he says that 'he is the head of all rule and authority' (Colossians 2:10) and then, speaking of his cross, he declares that there he 'disarmed the principalities and powers and made a public example of them' (2:15). So, as Creator, as Redeemer, as Victor, his supremacy is absolute. There may be many powers in the universe but there can be only one Lord, and all other powers exist only beneath his sovereign sway.

Son of God

The terms 'Lord' and 'Son of God' have something in common. Both of them are used in the New Testament in connexion with the deity of Jesus Christ. In fact, they are the two chief terms employed. They are also both terms of relationship. However, the relationship indicated by each is a different one. When we use the term 'Lord' we are thinking of the relationship of the Lord Jesus to the universe and to us. It is one of sovereignty and supremacy. He is in control of everything. The term 'Son of God', on the other hand, points to his relationship with God the Father. Both underline his deity, but they do it in different ways.

We noted some aspects of its New Testament use in chapters 2 and 3. There is no doubt, however, that the chief exposition of its meaning comes in the teaching of our Lord given in the gospel of John. We shall now concentrate on this.

The Lord Jesus used the terms 'Father' and 'son' in such a way as to suggest that the relationship between him and God was without any parallel. God is *the* Father and he is *the* Son (John 3:35; 5:19–27; etc.). He spoke of him as 'my Father', in a way which, to say the least, was not characteristic of Jewish practice. After the resurrection he said to Mary Magdalene, 'I am ascending to my Father and your Father' (John 20:17). Why not 'our Father'? This would have been more natural if he had not been aware of a special relationship with God. In fact, although he taught his disciples to address God this way in the Lord's Prayer, there is no evidence he ever prayed that prayer with them.

He clearly believed and taught that he had an existence in heaven before he ever came to earth. He said, for instance, 'I have come down from heaven, not to do my own will, but the will of him who sent me.' (John 6:38; cf. 3:13, 17; 6:33, 35, 50f., etc.) John 17:27f if particularly impressive. Here, in consecutive verses, he says he came from the Father. The first statement uses the Greek preposition *para*, which really means 'from the side of', but the second, *ek*, goes far beyond this in its meaning, for it means 'out of', and so suggests that the Son is from the very being of the Father. This then tells us something about his real nature and not simply about a previous existence. This too is suggested when he speaks of his glory with the Father before the very foundation of the world (John 17:5, 24).

There are some things that God and God alone is able to do. Only God can raise the dead to new life, only he can give eternal life, only he sits on the great throne to judge all men. All these Christ claimed to do (John 5:21–29), although not independently of the Father but as perfectly expressing his will. As we have seen earlier, he also claimed that he would take back his own life from the grave and so break the power of death (John 2:19–21; 10:17f.).

He said also that he was able to meet the very deepest needs of men. All those who came before him in Old Testament times pointed men to God as the answer to their needs, but he pointed men to himself. He promised to give them living water (John 4:10–14), the bread of life (John 6:27), in fact to be himself that bread (John 6:35), to set them completely free from slavery to sin (John 8:34–36) and to bestow both peace and joy on them (John 14:27; 15:11). Those who have put their trust in him know these claims are by no means idle and that every one of them is true.

One of his most staggering claims is linked with the words 'I am', which occur so frequently in the gospel of John. In this expression special emphasis in the Greek is placed on the pronoun. He and the Jews were talking together about Abraham. The Saviour said to them, 'Truly, truly, I say to you, before Abraham was, I am.' (John 8:58). Do you see what this implies? If he had wanted simply to indicate that he was pre-existent and therefore lived before Abraham (in itself a big claim) all he needed to say was, 'Before Abraham, I was.' But the words he actually used clearly reminded his hearers of the great revelation God made to Moses when he called himself 'I am' (Exodus 3:14). He was claiming to be God!

In this passage in Exodus, God also said 'I am who I am', which might perhaps be translated instead 'I will be what I will be'. It is as if he is saying to his people that he is going to show many different sides of his nature and his character to them throughout the years ahead. Perhaps this is what the Lord Jesus is himself saying when he says, 'I am the bread of life,' 'I am the way, the truth and the life,' 'I am the resurrection and the life,' and so on. All that his people need, that will he be to them as life proceeds.

John 18:1–8 records a most striking event. Soldiers had come into the garden of Gethsemane to take Jesus:

> Jesus ... said to them, 'Whom do you seek?' They answered him, 'Jesus of Nazareth.' Jesus said to them, 'I am he.' ... When he said to them, 'I am he,' they drew back and fell to the ground.

This incident is at first difficult to understand. It is the reaction of the soldiers that is so puzzling. Then we notice that Jesus used the majestic phrase 'I am', and that the word 'he' which follows it in some of our English versions is not in the original. Like several other passages in the gospel of John, the answer of Jesus can be understood at two levels. On the face of it, he is simply identifying himself as the man they are seeking. It may be, however, that he said the words with such majesty that they linked them with the great revelation of God in Exodus, and so fell to the ground.

Several times in this gospel we find the Jews taking up stones to stone him, and it was normally when they realized he was claiming to be divine (5:17f.; 8:58f; 10:30f.). In the last of these passages, Jesus was using the pastoral language of Palestine and applying it to his relationship with his disciples. He was the shepherd and they were the sheep. He would look after them and keep them safe. Then he says, 'My Father, who has given them to me, is greater than all, and no one is able to snatch them out of the Father's hand. I and the Father are one.' (John 10:29f.) It was at this point the Jews took up stones to stone him. Now what does the last statement of that quotation mean? The word 'one' is in the neuter gender in Greek. Jesus is not saying that he and the Father are one person. Is it enough simply to say – as some have said – that they are one in will or in purpose? This could perhaps imply that Jesus is different from Christians only in degree, that is in the extent of his submission to God's will. The passage must mean more than this. It is *power* which is being discussed. If he and the Father are one in power, this means the Lord Jesus is almighty, and if he is almighty he is God!

Space does not permit us to pursue this immensely rich topic much further, but if you want to do so yourself, you should read and ponder prayerfully the following passages from the gospel of John: 11:4; 12:44f.; 14:6–11, 23; 15:23f.; 16:3, 15.

It is possible that some reader will raise an objection at this point. We have been looking at many passages from the gospel of John, but what about the other gospels? Is it possible that John has 'cooked the books' and given us material he has constructed himself and which does not really show us the mind of the Lord Jesus? No, for the term 'Son of God' occurs in all four gospels, not just in one. There is one passage of special importance. In Matthew 11:27, the Saviour says, 'All things have been delivered to me by my Father; and no one knows the Son except the Father, and no one knows the Father except the Son and any one to whom the Son chooses to reveal him.' This passage, with its parallel in Luke 10:22, has been called 'a bolt from the Johannine blue'. Yet, although it sounds so Johannine, it is here in two of the synoptic gospels, and all attempts to dislodge it from the text have failed. The claims made by Jesus here are deeply impressive and are right along the same lines as the teaching we have found in the gospel of John.

Claims to be reckoned with

If the reader has been deeply interested in Jesus of Nazareth and has treated his teaching and character with respect, but has never worshipped him or committed his life to him, the facts themselves press upon him his obligation to surrender himself to the Saviour and to submit the whole of life to his lordship.

11

THE WONDER OF GOD INCARNATE

What are we to make of all the Bible tells us about the Lord Jesus Christ? The teaching of the various New Testament books is wonderful, but it raises all sorts of questions in our minds. This is just as it should be. Every major phenomenon in the universe has made human beings think deeply. The nature of life, the existence of evil, the meaning of suffering, all these and many more have kept philosophers busy since serious thought began, and a great many ordinary folk who would never claim to be philosophers have in fact thought about them quite deeply. It would be a great surprise if, assuming the Lord Jesus really is all he claimed to be, his presence in the world raised no questions or problems in our minds.

What sort of questions occur to us? Was he really both God and man at the same time or was he some being occupying a kind of intermediate position between the two? If he was in fact both God and man, did he stop being God when he became man? When he went back to heaven did he stop being man? Was he both God and man right from the beginning of his life, or was he raised to a higher level of existence at some point in time? If he was divine, how could he suffer, how could he be tempted? If he was human, how could he save helpless humans from their sins? God knows everything and is everywhere. A man grows in knowledge but is always more notable for his ignorance than for what he knows, and he can only be in one place at a time. How then could the Lord Jesus Christ possibly be both God and man at once?

These are just a few of the questions people have been asking

about him ever since his earthly life, and every one of them
is being asked today. It will be surprising if some of them are
not in your own mind. Now it would be interesting and helpful
for us to trace the history of debates about his person down
through the centuries. This would however fall outside the
purpose of our present volume, which is concentrating on what
the *Bible* teaches about him. What we can do, however, is to
come to the Bible with these questions in our minds, asking
to what extent God's word provides clues to their answers.

True God and perfect man

We do not need to expound this very fully as we have already
seen this over and over again. Just to emphasize the point,
however, take the teaching of the letter to the Hebrews. We
looked at this in chapter 2, but now we should think about its
significance. Paul, in Romans 9–11, deals with the vexed
question of the apparent rejection of the Jews by God. The
way he deals with it, at least in the first two of these chapters,
is simply to set side by side the two great facts which bear on
this, namely the sovereignty of God (Romans 9:1–29) and the
responsibility of men (9:30–10:21). Where the two meet and
how they relate to each other is a mystery, but Paul does not
deny either factor, but sets them alongside each other. Now
the writer to the Hebrews does just the same in relation to the
person of the Saviour in the first two chapters of his book. In
Hebrews 1:1 – 2:4 it is his deity which is in view, while in
2:5–18 it is his humanity.

Great terms like 'Son', 'Lord' and 'God' are used in the first
chapter, while in chapter 2 (verse 9) he uses for the first time
the name 'Jesus', the name of his humanity, the name his family
gave him at his birth. He is very interested in the high priesthood
of Jesus, and such an office could of course only be performed
by a real man. He has a lot to say also about his sufferings
and his temptations as qualifying him for his work (Hebrews
2:17f.; 4:14–16). He really understands what human life is like.
At the same time, it is to a throne of grace that we come, and

the one who sits on it is a king and the very Son of God. His humanity enables him to feel with us; his deity gives him power to help.

There is, in fact, one phrase used by the writer of this letter which perfectly sums up the two basic facts about his person. He is 'Jesus, the Son of God' (Hebrews 4:14). All the experience of his human life is in this phrase, and all the power and authority of the eternal Son of God.

One person

The New Testament really provides us with three basic facts about him, not just two. Not only was he both God and man; he was both of them at once. His unity therefore provides the third fact.

Psychologists often lay stress upon integration of personality. There is, of course, a pathological condition called schizophrenia, or split personality. This is a sad condition which raises great problems both for the sufferer and those who are brought into contact with him. There are also, of course, many people who have more than one 'personality' although not in this pathological sense. They are 'two-faced'. They present different faces to different people. They may do it quite deliberately. Sometimes they may hardly be aware of it.

Another defect in human beings is a lack of balance. This does not have to be extreme for us to recognize it. One man or woman may be very stern and strict in dealing with others, while another may be much too soft and pliable. There is a middle way between these extremes. A human being who is mature in character and in his or her relationships inspires great confidence in others.

What about the Lord Jesus Christ? Here we have a person with the most beautifully balanced character. In him holiness and love found their perfect point of integration. Moreover, he was always the same, and did not 'put on an act' before any group of people or any individual. Whether he was talking to his disciples, or to interested enquirers or was confronted by his bitterest foes, he was always the same. He was, in fact, before all kinds of people, exactly what he was before God. In his great 'high priestly prayer', recorded in John 17, he prays for his disciples, and so his true attitude to them stands revealed. There is absolutely no discord between what he said then in the place of prayer and what he said and did when he was with them. The same motives of love for God and love for men controlled all he ever did and said and prayed and was.

Now this perfect balance, this total integration, applied supremely to his deity and his humanity. We cannot go through the gospels distributing his deeds and words between the divine and human elements in him. We may be inclined to say that he performed his miracles as God and suffered and was tempted as man, but it is not as easy as that. Did he not stretch out a human hand to touch the leper when the divine power flowed from him in cleansing? Was it not divine as well as human love that kept him on the cross when his enemies were taunting him and yelling to him to come down? No doubt this raises problems for us, but the problems raised by driving this kind of wedge between the activities of his two natures are in fact even greater. Jesus was one person, although a person with divine and human characteristics. As H. E. W. Turner has put it (in *Jesus, Master and Lord*):

> The person of Jesus does not come apart in our hands into the two halves of humanity and divinity, one of which we have to set on one side when we begin to examine the other. His Personality is a seamless whole.

Before the incarnation

John, in the great prologue to his gospel, tells us that the eternal Word was both with God and was himself God (John 1:1). He then goes on to say, 'And the Word became flesh and dwelt among us, full of grace and truth.' (John 1:14). He had to become flesh, because he was not flesh when he was in heaven. He was in no sense man before the incarnation took place.

We must never lose sight of the fact that God and man are

very different. Yes, he made us in his image, but we must never 'make' him in ours. He is infinitely great, our eternal Creator. The Creator/creature distinction is never broken down. It is quite true that Peter says God has enabled us to be 'partakers of the divine nature' (2 Peter 1:4). Look at the context of this verse, however, and you will see very clearly that it is all about moral qualities. God does, through grace, impart qualities of his character to us, so that, as he is holy so we may pursue holiness, and something of his love and wisdom may be reproduced in us by the Holy Spirit. There are, however, many qualities of God which are never communicated to other beings, qualities like self-existence and omnipresence, the ability to be in all places at one time.

Why are we saying all this? In order to emphasize the distinction between the two natures of our Lord, so that we must not imagine the one contained the other before he came to earth. God created the world; it was not simply an extension of his own being. What a man creates is not himself although it may bear the marks of what he is. The very same is true of God.

Some early teachers maintained that the Son of God possessed 'heavenly flesh' (whatever that is!) before his birth, while others said he gained nothing from Mary, but she was merely the vehicle through whom he passed into the world. Both these ideas must be rejected. He became what he was not before he came; he became flesh, that is, human nature in its entirety, apart from sin. (As we have seen, the pre-incarnate manifestations of Jesus anticipate the incarnation, but are not real parallels to it.)

The very most we can say is that God, because he is God, always possessed the power to do what he actually did in the incarnation. At any time he could have assumed human nature and been born on earth. The timing of it was in line with his great purpose. As Paul puts it, 'When the time had fully come, God sent forth his Son, born of a woman, born under the law.' (Galatians 4:4.)

The virgin birth

The doctrine known as the virgin birth might be more accurately renamed the virgin conception, although the usual less exact expression is not really misleading. It is taught very clearly in the New Testament. It is true that the incarnation and the virgin birth are not identical, but they are very closely related. The incarnation is the *fact* that God became man, while the virgin birth is the *method* by which this took place.

Some have objected that it is only Matthew and Luke who record this fact. But it is, after all, only the gospels which record the facts about the life of Jesus. The epistles contain inspired meditations on those facts. The other two gospels have precluded reference to the virgin birth by starting the story at the beginning of his ministry, not at the start of his life, although John takes us right into eternity in his prologue. It is noticeable too that the other New Testament writers say nothing that militates against this doctrine. In fact, some passages might just suggest a knowledge of it (e.g. Galatians 4:4). It is well worth noting that the only gospel writer who uses the term 'his parents' in relation to Jesus is Luke, who has provided against misinterpretation of this conventional expression already by recording the virgin birth.

Matthew, in a way so characteristic of him, relates the virgin birth to the Old Testament. He quotes the words of Isaiah, 'Behold, a virgin shall conceive and bear a son, and his name shall be called Emmanuel,' and then adds this comment: 'which means, God with us.' (Matthew 1:23.) So the virgin birth was an element in the Old Testament prediction of the Messiah.

Luke records a most impressive statement from the angel Gabriel, in his conversation with Mary before the birth of the Saviour. 'The Holy Spirit will come upon you, and the power of the Most High will overshadow you; therefore the child to be born will be called holy, the Son of God.' (Luke 1:35.) The word 'therefore' is always worth noting when it occurs in Scripture, but there can be few examples of it that are more important than this. The Lord Jesus was born into a sinful race,

but he was not sinful. He was conceived by the Holy Spirit
(cf. Matthew 1:20). He was truly divine, and yet he was truly
'the child', and therefore human.

We may ask all sorts of questions about chromosomes and
DNA, and so on, but the fact remains that man is God's creature
and the whole process of birth is one he ordained. The Holy
Spirit, himself divine, was supervising everything just as he did
at the very creation of the universe (Genesis 1:2). The records
do not set out to answer all our questions, but the facts are
there. He was divine, he was holy, he was sinless. Humanity
without sin had been seen once before – in Adam and Eve before
they disobeyed God. Now such humanity was seen again, but
this time in a perfect man who was also truly divine. In chapter
2 we made some reference to what is known as adoptionism.
This is the idea, which keeps on recurring at different periods
in church history, that Jesus was not the eternal Son of God.
He started life as a man, but at some point or other he 'became'
the Son of God, because he had been so obedient to God.
Adoptionists have not agreed as to the particular point in time
when this happened. Some identified his baptism as the
moment, others his resurrection, while others thought of this
'deification' as going on gradually throughout his life, to be
completed at his resurrection.

Such a view cannot stand scrutiny in the full light of the
New Testament teaching. All that we have seen of its teaching
on his divine pre-existence militates against it. Jesus Christ was
both God and man from the very beginning of his earthly
existence, even before he became visible as a distinct person
and was still in the womb of his mother. This is why it is
important to emphasize that this was a virgin *conception*.

Some views of the Lord Jesus are in danger of viewing him
as if he were different only in degree from the Christian. It is
the glory of the gospel that forgiveness brings the life of God
right into the soul of man, so that the Christian is 'in Christ'
and Christ is in him. He is indwelt by the living God himself.
This is not, however, what the New Testament teaches us about
Christ. God was not simply in Christ (even though that state-

ment is not objectionable simply as it stands) but he was incarnate in Christ. God actually became a man in Christ, he did not just indwell a man. God and man were not just united in fellowship, or in purpose, they were united absolutely. They constituted one person.

This means that a nature which can neither diminish nor develop was joined to a nature in the raw, a nature destined, like every human nature, to grow physically and to mature intellectually, emotionally and in other ways. Now at every stage of this development he was the God-man. The man is not more human than the child nor the child than the baby, nor even the baby than the foetus. The human nature is complete as a nature at every stage, although it is developing constantly, just as the oak tree does from the acorn. We can cut a section so to speak, at any point in our Lord's life from the womb to the tomb (and even, as we shall see, beyond the tomb) and say, 'This is God; this is also man.'

He emptied himself

A term that is often used in connexion with Christology is *kenosis*, a Greek word meaning 'emptying'. The reason for its use is that Paul employs the corresponding verb in Philippians 2:7. It comes within the body of a glorious passage, which the RSV translates as follows (Philippians 2:5–8):

> Have this mind among yourselves, which you have in Christ Jesus, who, though he was in the form of God, did not count equality with God a thing to be grasped, but emptied himself, taking the form of a servant, being born in the likeness of men. And being found in human form he humbled himself and became obedient unto death, even death on a cross.

We will stop at that point meantime, but will look at the remainder of it later in this chapter (page 123).

What was this kenosis? Some have suggested that Jesus emptied himself of his divine qualities, or at least certain of them, when he became a man, and that this is what Paul means here. This is highly doubtful, to say the least. It is doubtful on general grounds. How can God divest himself of some of his qualities and remain God? A being who is not all-powerful, all-knowing and present everywhere is just not God. God as he is made known to us in his word has all these qualities and we can no more conceive him without them than we can conceive matter without form and substance.

But we are not left to general considerations. The idea does not properly fit the passage. Verse 6 speaks of equality, verse 7 of service and between the two ideas comes the self-emptying. Moreover, verse 8 is also controlled by the ideas of humility and obedience, which are intimately related to the role of a servant. In the focal verse itself, Paul says that he emptied himself, *taking* the form of a servant. What he surrendered for the time being was his equality with God, to replace this with the role of a humble and obedient servant.

This means that the passage is not about the setting aside of powers but about the willingness to obey. In fact the word translated 'servant' really means 'bondslave'. He placed himself under the Law (Galatians 4:4). He said, 'I seek not my own will, but the will of him who sent me.' (John 5:30.) Later, he declared, 'I have come down from heaven, not to do my own will, but the will of him who sent me.' (John 6:38.) When the terms of that will pressed so hard upon him in the garden of Gethsemane, his utter surrender to it was expressed in the words, 'Not my will, but thine, be done.' (Luke 22:42.) In fact, the whole record of the gospels could provide us with a commentary on this Philippian passage.

If then it was the Father's will that governed every action of life, it was that will which controlled his use of his divine powers. During his ministry he multiplied loaves and fishes, but during the temptation in the wilderness he would not turn stones into bread. The first was his Father's plan; the second was contrary to it.

Mention of the temptations will undoubtedly raise important questions in the mind of many a reader. Did he face these temptations as man or as the God-man, and if the latter does

THE WONDER OF GOD INCARNATE

this mean he used his divine powers? If so, then surely his experience of temptation was not truly human? Without doubt, there is a lot of confused thinking about this issue. It is quite true that the emphasis in the temptation narratives is upon his humanity. Both Matthew 4 and Luke 4 show him using passages from Deuteronomy, and taking the place of a man under the will of God. In other words, he truly acted as a servant of God during this experience of temptation. Yet he was God as well as man. The factor that is so often overlooked is that *nobody* can face temptation without the power of God. I cannot, you cannot, and neither could Jesus. He was not using powers unavailable to us, because the gospel triumphantly proclaims that God's power is available to us also when we face the tempter.

Perhaps the key to the problem of Jesus' knowledge lies here. He said that he did not know the date of his second advent (Mark 13:32). Yet, if he was God, he must have known everything. How can absolute knowledge and limited knowledge co-exist? An idea that has helped me arises from the fact that none of us ever uses as much knowledge as he possesses. Most of the knowledge we have is not present to our conscious minds. Consciousness is like a very small tip of a very large iceberg. It is our conscious knowledge that we are aware of using. If I have learned something in the past and yet it is hidden in my subconscious mind at the moment awaiting the appropriate stimulus before it can come into my consciousness, can I be said to know it? In a sense I do and in a sense I do not. Perhaps such items as these were below the level of Jesus' consciousness so that, at that moment, for purposes of conscious action, he could not be said to know them, and yet they were present in the great unlimited reservoir of divine knowledge which was in union with his human nature. I cannot give you biblical chapter and verse for this, but it has helped me.

Mysteriously, it seems necessary for us to say that, in some sense, Christ was still present everywhere even while he was present on earth. This is very difficult to understand. Perhaps the key to it lies in an analysis of what we mean by the term 'present'. God is present in his universe in different ways. It is true that he is present everywhere, upholding the whole universe from within. It is also true that he was present in a special sense on Mount Sinai and in the Temple at Jerusalem. It is also true that he is present in an even more special way in the heart of the Christian. He was present in the most special way of all in Christ, in fact, in a way that was completely without parallel. If some of these modes could be true simultaneously, as they clearly were, why not the first and the last?

Indwelt by the Holy Spirit

At this point it is helpful to remember the function of the Holy Spirit in the life of Jesus. The Spirit was related to Jesus in his deity, because of their unity in the triune life of God. This relationship was eternal. He was also related to him in his humanity, because the Lord Jesus was filled with the Spirit (Luke 4:1).

Christians have sometimes debated whether Jesus did his miracles in virtue of his own divine power or in the power of the Holy Spirit. You can make out a case for each. Jesus said, 'If it is by the Spirit of God that I cast out demons, then the kingdom of God has come upon you.' (Matthew 12:28.) Does that settle it? Remember that after his first miracle, John tells us, 'This, the first of his signs, Jesus did at Cana in Galilee, and manifested his glory; and his disciples believed in him.' (John 2:11; cf. John 20:30f.) Surely both sides are right! His divine powers were exercised under the constant control of the Holy Spirit. In a Christian, submission to God's will and the fullness of the Spirit belong together. This was surely true also of Jesus.

In practical terms, this presumably meant that it was the Spirit who restrained the exercise of Jesus' divine powers in the 'silent years' before his ministry began. Except in character and in his sense of special relationship to God (Luke 2:41–52) he would be an ordinary intelligent child. Then from his baptism onwards, those powers would be exercised in his special ministry, but only as God's purpose determined this and so only under the control of the Holy Spirit.

Does this mean that Jesus' human experience was just like that of the Christian? Yes and no! He was one with us because divine power was channelled into his human life through the mediation of the Holy Spirit (cf. Luke 4:14 and Ephesians 3:20). He was unlike us because the true source of this power was in his own divine being, while for us, the power of God is a gift of his grace, his favour which we do not deserve (2 Corinthians 12:9). Incarnation (God becoming man) is the key to the first, indwelling (God living in man) the key to the second. This makes him truly human and yet truly divine.

He is exalted

The exaltation of the Lord Jesus can be viewed from two different and yet complementary angles. From the standpoint of his divine nature it was simply the restoration of that glory which was his before the world was (John 17:5, 24). This does not mean, of course, that he now acts independently whereas in the days of his flesh he only acted under instructions from his Father. It is important to remember that there is never, in heaven or on earth, any division of purpose between the Father and the Son. The distinctive thing about his human life is that this oneness of purpose was expressed under human conditions of life, requiring him to render a human obedience to the Father.

From the standpoint of his humanity, it is the exaltation of his human nature. In the great Philippian passage, Paul, having spoken of Christ's obedience to death, goes on to say (Philippians 2:9–11):

Therefore God has highly exalted him and bestowed on him the name that is above every name, that at the name of Jesus every knee should bow, in heaven and on earth and under the earth, and every tongue confess that Jesus Christ is Lord, to the glory of God the Father.

This means that we need to think of Jesus as man still. Glorified humanity is still humanity. Christians are going to be glorified, but we shall not cease to be human because of it. This is a wonderful fact. It means that we can come to him, confident that he understands exactly what human life with all its pressures and temptations and sufferings is like. He has gone deeper in terms of each of these than any of us will ever go. So his sympathy and human understanding are full ranging. At the very same time he is God and so has all the resources to come to our aid.

In a family, one parent is often the child's refuge for sympathy and the other for strength. In Christ the two are combined and carried to the highest power, in fact multiplied by infinity. How wonderful is he!

12

JESUS AND YOU

Throughout this book we have been surveying the teaching of the Bible about Jesus Christ. This teaching is deeply impressive. It is given through a great many different writers. Their books differ much in literary type, in style and in vocabulary. An extremely wide variety of words and phrases is used by the Bible writers to try to convey to their readers the meaning of his person. Nothing is stereotyped. Yet, despite this, there is an amazing consistency about the teaching of the Bible concerning him. It all fits together into a beautiful pattern.

It has been said that what marks out a true work of art in any medium, be it pencil, paint, stone, wood, cloth, language or music, is the fact that you may come to it time and time again and always find some new beauty in it. This makes the Bible God's own great work of art, and the nature of its subject is unmistakable. It is a portrait of the Lord Jesus Christ. Every book of the Bible adds its own brush strokes. Moreover, it is not simply a canvas portrait. It is not even a piece of sculpture. To say that the portrayal of Christ given in the Bible is three-dimensional is totally inadequate. To all the dimensions of earth is added the infinite dimension of heaven.

Yet even the concept of a work of art hardly does justice to the Bible presentation of Christ. An artist known to me told me how the artistic stimulus first came to him. As a child he was taken to the municipal art gallery in Glasgow. He enjoyed his visit and liked many of the pictures he saw. But then at last he stood before Rembrandt's *Man in Armour*. He was overcome with awe. He said to me, 'I felt this was not a portrait of the man, but the man himself.' It is Christ himself who confronts us within the Bible. We see him with the inner eye, we hear his voice with an inner ear. We cannot escape the challenge of the one who is not dead but lives for evermore, and whose majesty and glory and yet winsome humanness meet us in living power throughout the pages of Scripture.

What then is Christ for us today, or, to make it more specific and personal, what is he to you? This question has to be faced and answered by us all. He is too unique and compelling a figure to be ignored.

Someone to trust

One of the saddest aspects of our present society is the widespread breakdown of trust between human beings. Society can only function properly on a basis of confidence in others. Family life, business life, national and international life all run into great trouble when trust is undermined. What the economists call confidence in the pound or the dollar is really confidence in the British or the Americans whose actions determine the true value of their currency.

The enormous increase in the divorce rate speaks to us all too eloquently about this. Think of the colossal breakdown in confidence that lies behind most divorces, the deceit, the suspicion, the anxiety, the agony, all of which are either causes or symptoms of the destruction of trust between a husband and wife. In this sort of environment is it any wonder we are producing a generation that contains so many young people who feel they cannot really trust anybody?

If that is the kind of person you are − or even if it is not − Christ comes to you first of all as somebody to be trusted. He was constantly calling men to trust, which is really what the Biblical verb 'to believe' means. But you have perhaps learned from life's bitter experiences that it is not wise to trust anybody, and certainly not without evidence of trustworthiness. Christ produces evidence so full, so persuasive, so deeply moving, that it should sweep away all your reservations, all your cynicism. The Bible shows him to be somebody who always put others before himself, who never made promises and failed to keep them, who showed depths of compassion and tenderness which outclass every other human being in history. Yet at the same time, he was so strong that people knew they could lean on him as hard as they wanted, and he would prove as steady and firm as a rock.

The final evidence of the fact that he is to be trusted comes to us in the central events of the story, in his sufferings and death and resurrection. He had dealt with disease and demon-possession and death. Now he would get to the root of the entire human problem and deal with sin itself by bearing it and the divine punishment it so justly deserved. Here is the final self-forgetfulness and the purest love. And beyond it lay the triumph of the resurrection and all the power of new life.

Trust is the only proper response to such a person, and not simply trust in this statement or that promise, nor for this purpose or that. The trust for which he calls is full confidence in him, to save me from sin, to guide me in life, to receive me to heaven. Faith grows as it considers its object, and as it sees more and more clearly how trustworthy he is in one sphere after another, but it cannot grow until it is born, and it is born in commitment to him. Why should you not make that commitment now without delay? The rest of the chapter will be even more meaningful to you if you have first trusted yourself to him.

Someone to thank

An atheist who was converted to Christ said that one of the worst features of being an atheist is that you have nobody to thank. Surrounded by blessings untold and attributing them all to nature or to the life-force or to evolution, and just nobody to thank! How different for the Christian! He starts off by giving thanks to the Lord Jesus for saving him from his sins. To him this is the supremely wonderful thing that has made everything look different.

Then he discovers that the Christ who has saved him from sin is able to keep him from sin, because he now lives within him, and so he gives thanks for this. Then he finds that he guides him through the Bible when he has problems, that he gives him power to speak about him to other people, and that he has promised to come back again to conduct him to heaven. All these facts add further notes or even movements to the great symphony of thanksgiving which is beginning to take shape.

His thanksgiving takes on more and more dimensions. He discovers that Christ is the Creator of the universe, so that he can thank him for material as well as for spiritual blessings. He discovers that the element of meaning in everything he sees is really derived from him who is the Word and the Wisdom of God.

Even troubles and problems and afflictions cannot rob him of his gratitude, for in them all he can see a divine thread of purpose. He knows that although they are not pleasant and he would rather be without them, Christ is on the throne of the universe and he has allowed them to come into life so that he can give him strength in adversity, comfort in sorrow, and courage in the face of danger.

Someone to love

Human life is all about relationships. All of us know in our heart of hearts, no matter how materialistic we may be, that it is people who really matter and not things. That is really what the songs are all about, what the books are all about, what life is all about. If trust is a vitally important feature of human relationships, so is love. This word is used today so often as if it simply meant sexual love, and even then largely in terms of its physical side. Yet we all know that love is only worthy of that name when it is not self-seeking but self-denying and is concerned with the well-being of the person who is its object.

A good many songs have been written about unrequited love. It is a sad experience. The Son of God knows more about this than any other person. As he surveyed the city that would crucify him in just a few days, he cried out (Matthew 23:37):

> O Jerusalem, Jerusalem, killing the prophets and stoning those who are sent to you! How often would I have gathered your children together as a hen gathers her brood under her wings, and you would not!

Other songs have been written about a lover who proves unfaithful, whose love does not last or proves to be too self-centred. Some of us do not show much love unless we are loved in return. Our 'love' is more like a kind of blackmail to secure the attention of somebody else. Christ knows much about this too. His love is always pure, strong, persistent and utterly selfless, but he often poured and pours it out on those who give so little in return.

Love like that deserves and ought to have wholehearted, life-long devotion from you and me. If through trust you have been brought into a new relationship with him, then all the conditions are there for an ever-deepening outpouring of love and devotion to him. His love for you does not vary. It is always absolute. If you trust him, and you ponder with thankfulness all he has done for you, then your love for him will grow and grow until it is the deepest fact of your life.

Someone to serve

Psychologists tell us that the best way to a truly integrated personality and therefore to a satisfying life, is to find the centre of life outside oneself. Paradoxically, if we lose ourselves in serving a cause or a person, we find ourselves. Self-centredness makes for utter misery and is, both in itself and in its effects, a foretaste of hell.

Now the Lord Jesus Christ is one who calls us to serve him. He gives us work to do. Nothing could be a greater privilege. Not only what we think of as Christian service, activities like leading a service, preaching a sermon, singing in the choir, teaching a Sunday-school class, is service for Christ. Everything we do throughout the whole of life, down to the last detail of it, should be seen as service for him. In fact, to view life this way often leads to a drastic reappraisal of our sense of priorities.

It may be that you have never really thought about the claims of Christ upon your time and talents. If you are a Christian, it is not up to you to choose the course of your life, to decide what job you will do or how you will spend your leisure time. That is for him to decide. Ask him to show you and give yourself a chance to listen to what he says through the Bible and in prayer, and you will not lack the direction you need. It will not all come at once, but you can trust him to show you each stage of the pathway as you need to walk it.

Obedience is of vital importance in the Christian life. Some Christians ransack the Bible looking for promises and hardly give a thought to the commands staring them in the face on every page. The promises are given to enable us to carry out the commands. We shall not lack anything, for his service brings the truest fulfilment to those who serve him.

Someone to worship

It is possible that somebody reading this chapter has an uncomfortable feeling. All that has been said may be true, but is it not possible for us, in each of these ways, to be still very much self-centred and self-occupied?

Take faith, for example. Perhaps our real aim in putting our trust in Christ is to get something for ourselves, something the Bible calls 'salvation'. We discover that thanksgiving makes us feel good and we enjoy the feeling. Love secures that we are loved ourselves and we may be doing our service for the 'perks', for what we may get out of it.

Now we may think these objections are a bit cynical, but they are not without point. It is possible to be self-centred in all these areas, so that we are really using Christ as a means to an end, and not treating him as an end in himself. The thought is horrifying. Martin Buber used to talk about the difference between an 'I – it' and an 'I – thou' relationship. In the first we really treat a human being as if he were less than human.

We treat him as a means to an end. In the second we establish a true relationship which involves respect for the other's person-hood.

Now our relationship with Christ should be the greatest 'I – Thou' relationship of life. In fact, it might be better to call it the 'Thou – I' relationship. He does not exist to serve ends determined by our wants and needs. We exist to serve ends determined by him. What saves our trust, our gratitude, our love and our service from being completely vitiated by self, is the fact that they are all seen in the context of worship. We see that the Christ who offers himself to us is God and Lord. He is worthy and we are worthless. He will be the centre of the worship of the redeemed universe throughout all eternity and we shall take our place among the worshippers. Perhaps in heaven we may be hardly aware that we exist. What will dominate everything is the fact that he exists, and that he is all-holy, all-wise, all-loving. Worthy is his name!

FURTHER READING

From the wealth of material available, the following books are recommended if you would like to study further. They are listed roughly in order of simplicity of approach, commencing with the simplest.

L. Morris, *The Lord from Heaven* (Inter-Varsity Press).
A. M. Stibbs, *God became Man* (Tyndale House).
M. Green (ed.), *The Truth of God Incarnate* (Hodder & Stoughton).
H. D. McDonald, *Jesus: Human and Divine* (Pickering & Inglis).
G. Carey, *God Incarnate* (Inter-Varsity Press).
H. P. Liddon, *The Divinity of our Lord and Saviour Jesus Christ* (Rivingtons).
G. C. Berkouwer, *The Person of Christ* (Inter-Varsity Press).

INDEX